SWINGING for the FENCES

Hi Don:

merry Christmas. You don't really have to read this but you will be tested on it later ☺.

Paul

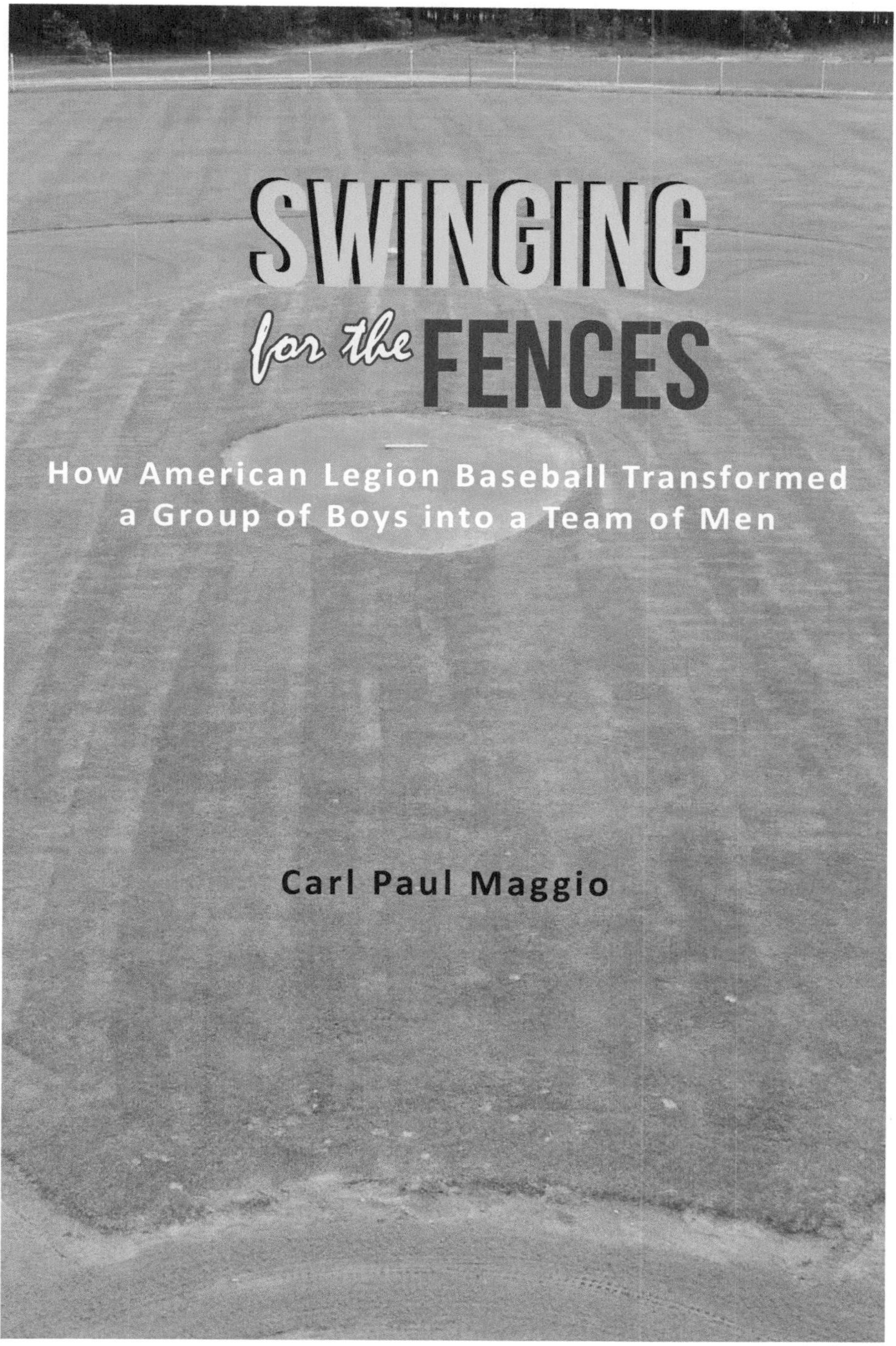
SWINGING
for the FENCES
How American Legion Baseball Transformed
a Group of Boys into a Team of Men
Carl Paul Maggio

Swinging for the Fences: How American Legion Baseball Transformed a Group of Boys into a Team of Men

Published by Wheatmark®
1760 East River Road, Suite 145, Tucson, Arizona 85718 U.S.A.
www.wheatmark.com

ISBN: 978-1-62787-003-0 (paperback)
ISBN: 978-1-62787-023-8 (ebook)
LCCN: 2013941842

rev201301

This book is about living one's life in full consciousness and existing with integrity and respect toward your fellow earth dwellers. You judge a person's life by what they leave us as their legacy, and my dedicatee left behind nothing but love and happiness. My instincts and knowledge of the man told me he wanted this book to be written. The book offers little speculation and everything to discover.

So I dedicate this book to William Angelo Consolo, his family, and all my other teammates who became blood brothers during the magical summer of 1951.

The author and The Legend

In Memory of My Georgie The legend: George "Sparky" Anderson

ON NOVEMBER 4, 2010, ABOUT two weeks after this book was completed, George "Sparky" Anderson passed on to a higher spiritual dimension. It was a sad and unforgettable day for me and my seven remaining teammates. His passing ended our earthly sixty-five-year-old love relationship with him.

Sparky's departure was thirty-one months after his best friend, Billy Consolo, abruptly left us. They are up there somewhere playing catch together once again, with an incredibly shiny new baseball.

Have fun boys!!
Carl Paul Maggio

Contents

Members of the 1951 American Legion Baseball champions and friends at the 2005 reunion

FOREWORD BY GEORGE "SPARKY" ANDERSON

TODAY, BASEBALL IS NOT THE same game it was in 1951. Then again, the world is not the same place either. That summer of 1951, which my friend Carl captures so well in this book, is a magical time from a bygone era. We were a ragtag bunch of seventeen-year-old kids who found out that once in a while it is possible to do the impossible, if only you can put your best foot forward.

As I look back on my life in baseball, there are three things that really stand out to me as memorable events. One, of course, was being inducted into the Baseball Hall of Fame in 2000. Another was being inducted into the University of Southern California Hall of Fame. The third, and perhaps the most nostalgic of memories, was winning the American Legion World Series in 1951. You might think that my three World Series wins would beat that, but when you experience something like that as the green kid that I was, nothing can quite compare. It is really quite astounding to think that we outshone 16,299 teams to come out on top of it all. It was pure teamwork fueled by pure adrenaline. What a great memory and what a great way to begin a baseball career as a kid just starting out.

Sadly, there are now only ten of us left from that original team of 1951. They were and are a wonderful bunch of guys, and I am so thrilled that they will live on through the pages of this book. I'm so glad the rest of the world will get to know Carl, Billy, and the rest of the gang as I have, doing what they loved best—playing baseball.

I know that the spirit of Billy Consolo was a guiding force behind this book, and I am so happy to see our friendship celebrated here. The moment we met we became like brothers, as close as two people could ever get. Since his passing, he has been in my thoughts and prayers without fail.

I am also happy to see our coach, Benny Lefebvre, resurrected here. He deserves to be remembered and celebrated as the great man he was, influencing and shaping our young lives in unimaginable ways. He was the kind of role model who was unwaveringly kind, yet at the same time strict, always demanding more of us than we thought we had. He taught us a whole new way to play the game—his way. As much as we may have resisted that at first, it would ultimately shape all our professional and personal lives. Benny taught us how to be winners, both on and off the field.

I would love to have all those guys around me just one more time, for one more ice cold beer and a toast to the good old days. They're always here in my heart, that's for sure. Here's to you, fellas …

Love to all,

George "Sparky" Anderson

Acknowledgments

A BOOK WRITTEN BY A FIRST-TIME author is rarely completed without external support and this body of work is no exception. I would like to take this space to salute and express my gratitude to the people who made this factual creation possible. Each of you, in your own way, motivated me to write about my entertaining childhood experiences. I humbly thank you from the bottom of my heart and hope you will take personal pride in the success of this book.

To my brother-in-law, Tom Fish, thank you for tweaking my memory of our growing up together in Los Angeles. Your vivid memories of the details recapturing our amazing childhood and adolescence were truly invaluable to me and my writing process.

Terrie Frankel, your loving friendship and support of my writing style was instrumental in finishing the manuscript. You pushed me to complete what I had started … Thank you.

Nicole Dean, you were my teacher and mentor in steering me toward the proper artistic path. Without you, *Swinging for the Fences* would not have been a comprehensive narrative! Thanks to you, it became an amusing novel. You took my hand and guided me through it. My heartfelt thanks to you!

Cynthia Richmond, thank you for your expert editing and professional advice that helped me with the emotional aspects of my story. You also taught me to have patience with the development of my writing ability.

Rob Bernhagen, many thanks for your ideas and for helping

me understand what it was like to become an author. You led me along the way.

My loving thanks to my fantastic children Paul, Joela, and Ami and my six beautiful granddaughters Emma, Rachel, Addy, Ellina, Cecilia, and Meilee for your love and faith in my ability to get this project done. Without your patient, loving encouragement and undying confidence in me, my literary effort would never have come to fruition! Thank you for understanding my times of non-communication during the writing process.

Also, I must acknowledge and thank you, Billy Consolo. You sat on my shoulder the entire time the manuscript was being written and whispered in my ear. Without your influence and insistence this labor of love would never have been started, much less finished. I know you're up there somewhere smiling now that our mission is completed.

Thanks to everyone else who encouraged and wished me well in writing this important and compelling piece of my life.

I wish to acknowledge and thank Suzha Linch for the Sedona Photography; the shots of Secret Mesa are hers.

And last, but not least, I want to thank all of my American Legion teammates who provided input, dialogue, and unending support: George "Sparky" Anderson, Don Kenway, Warren Johnson, Mel Goldberg, Jerry Siegert, Bill Lachemann, Paul Schulte, and Frank Layana.

Prologue

IN THE 1940S, BASEBALL HAD a childlike innocence about it that captivated boys and adults alike. There were no monetary incentives that drew players from all over the world to get rich playing baseball. During the summer months the only amateur league available was American Legion Baseball. It was designed for boys aged seventeen and younger to polish their baseball skills and participate because they loved the game. Every boy on every playground in America wanted to play summer baseball on an organized team, so there were thousands of teams in 1951 scattered around the country wearing uniforms furnished by the American Legion—16,300 to be exact.

These teams turned out future major league players by the hordes. Our cast of performers was produced from Rancho La Cienaga playground in South Central Los Angeles, California. Playing baseball in California at that time was comparable to going to church. Everyone did it. We were living in an unworldly period in which people played an innocent game just for the love of it. Imagine that!

Our Legion team made history that magical lengthy summer of 1951 as we frolicked and bonded together in a way that extended our family tree. We were attached to each other like brothers and would remain that way for life. We attained a praiseworthy conclusion from playing baseball that long summer but none was more important than the lifelong relationships we cultivated alongside each other.

INTRODUCTION

BILLY CONSOLO AND I WERE lifelong friends for nearly sixty years and played baseball together as boys for about ten years. At seventeen years of age, we played on an American Legion Team with a group of playground and schoolmate friends and competed with 16,299 other teams nationally. Billy was the one person on our team whom we most depended upon to help us through baseball's and life's challenges.

The American Legion Baseball National program was well-organized and well-funded and gave young teenagers a chance to hone their athletic skills. At that time, most of the major leaguers had played their amateur baseball through the American Legion baseball system.

As a major league baseball player and coach, Billy led a charmed life until his untimely demise in March of 2008. His professional sports life consisted of ten years playing in the big leagues and seventeen years coaching, a total of twenty-seven years in the majors.

When I heard the disturbing news of his death, I was pulled out of my routine life instantly. I sat down to write a cathartic journal about coming to terms with Billy's death. After struggling for words for some time on my computer, suddenly the log jam opened and my journal became an automatic writing experience. I had no intention to write more than a three- or four-page reflection of my anger concerning his leaving so abruptly; however, the words flowed onto my computer monitor like my fingers were attached to my brain. I didn't need to think of what was being written, it just came out naturally and rapidly. During my writing, I felt Billy's presence throughout the entire composition of this manuscript.

I will never be able to shake the image of Billy's smiling face and gregarious personality that drew us together as young boys; however, this book is not about just one person or one team. It's about the great game of baseball and all those who played the game and learned its life lessons. I pray that this memoir will be a legacy, not only to the sixteen players who played on our American Legion team, but to the game of baseball as it once was played—for the love of the game.

—Carl Paul Maggio, 2013

The team members of the Crenshaw Post 715

Billy Consolo, one of the two who made the big leagues

1

THE THREE ACES

PEOPLE SAY THAT LIFE IS a game, and all we have to do is learn how to play it. If that is true, then perhaps it is a poker game with every player holding different cards drawn from the deck. Everyone gets dealt a different hand, and it's not always fair. Some get deuces while others get an ace or two. Whatever you get, you just play your hand the best you can at any given time. As for me, I'd have to say I've drawn pretty good cards. Oh, of course, there have been trials and disappointments along the way, but, all in all, not a bad hand.

I've been lucky enough to have drawn some aces, not least of which is a great childhood. At the time, I had no idea just how lucky that was, taking it for granted as kids are apt to do. But now, many decades older and wiser, I know exactly how important a happy childhood is in providing a foundation to build a life upon, free of the self-doubt and confusion that comes with a troubled childhood. Of course, I owe this to my parents, who were solid, hardworking people. Cut from the immigrant cloth that has defined so many American families, they were kind but never overindulgent. My needs were met abundantly, but I was never spoiled or coddled. All they wanted for me was a life that was a little bit better than their own.

Perhaps the luckiest child is not only born into good circumstance, but also at the right time. I enjoyed this good fortune, growing up in the 1930s, '40s, and '50s. This was the pre- and postwar era, a time when the electric excitement of American promise still lingered in the air for all to feel. The setting for me was Los Angeles, but not the smog-filled, traffic-congested city you might think of today. In that day, vestiges of LA's original paradise still remained. Yes, the cars, the tract housing, and the freeways had begun to make their mark, but there were still open spaces to be found and clean air to be inhaled. In those days, kids could run free, exploring and playing to their hearts' content. Not so anymore.

The third ace in my hand is, in my mind, the most important of all—good friends. My friends have been like a magic carpet, taking me to wonderful lands filled with excitement and laughter. The best friends I've ever had I met when I was still just a kid. Each of them got their own set of cards to play in life, which led them in various directions, but through the years we have always found ways to come back together and to keep in touch. In the storms of life, there is perhaps no better anchor than to know there are guys out there that have your back.

There are a couple of my childhood companions that particularly stand out in my mind like the hero and the sidekick in a Saturday matinee. In the game of life, they had been dealt their hands from a whole different deck of cards. They got cards the rest of us don't even get to touch, cards that gave them special access to the gods. There is no sense in feeling jealous about it or in trying to grab those cards for yourself. All you can do is stand back and watch in awe.

Billy Consolo was one of those golden boys who was given something beyond the gifts and talents of ordinary mortals. He was issued not just one of these special cards, but two. If I had to imagine what these cards looked like, I would imagine the image of Babe Ruth on one, sitting there among the clouds in heaven with a golden crown on his head and jewel-encrusted baseball equipment at his feet. On the other card, there might be an image of the Blarney stone sitting in its castle and shining as brightly as the sun.

Billy had been given the gift of godlike baseball ability. He could outplay most men before he was even a teen. What position did he play? You name it. He could catch, throw, pitch, run, and hit at a higher level than the merely talented players.

The cosmic card dealer also decided to give Billy the gift of charm combined with the gift of gab. No matter how much he talked, people loved to listen. He was the kind of guy who could tell a joke, and it didn't matter how bad the joke was, his audience was right there with him. Before he even got to the punch line, they were on the floor rolling with laughter.

Billy's sidekick was a kid named George Anderson, who would later be known to millions as "Sparky." His hand of cards was not especially notable, except for one. On George's special card, there might be the image of a bulldog, sitting there pugnaciously with its lower jaw jutting out and its eyes staring you down. With this card came a bottomless well of tenacity and a gut full of unbreakable will. He was also given the gift of simple immigrant parents who taught him that love and kindness were the greatest attributes one could possess.

With these sorts of guys, it is easy to imagine that they are immortal. They seem so much like the gods of Olympus that you think they have all the same attributes. You wouldn't expect them to vanish any more than the sun or the stars. And yet they all inevitably do. Like a shooting star, they light up the sky and then disappear, and you are left in the dark, wondering what happened.

• • • • • • • • • •

THE MAJESTIC FORM OF CATHEDRAL Rock reflected the dawn's muted golden glow, lit by daybreak's first light. Soft white clouds drifted across the blue sky behind the rocks, contrasting the earthy redness of the bold formations. The clouds puffed up like balloons and then dispersed as they passed over the high desert community of Sedona, Arizona.

We were there at the most beautiful time of year. Fall is the most celebrated season in this photogenic, high-desert wonderland, providing a reprieve between the long, hot summers and the chilly winters. Yet, the annual monsoon season had lingered well into autumn of the year, and black clouds were forming on the distant horizon.

I had first visited this beautiful place many decades earlier when I was only twenty-five years old. Los Angeles was no longer the place I had known as a boy, and I had made my way through the twists and turns of life to the hot, flat city of Phoenix to make a living and raise a family.

I worked as a rep for a line of ladies' swimwear, and one day I received a call from a lady running a store in a small town called Sedona. I looked on the map to find the small dot triangulated between the more familiar haunts of Prescott and Flagstaff. Getting in my car to make my way to the town, I expected nothing more than what I would have found in any of the dozens of dusty, half-abandoned small towns littered across Arizona.

The trip at first provided the usual Arizona scenery—wide open vistas with gently sloping hills covered with brown shrubs, cacti of various shapes and sizes, and tall, dry grasses waving in the wind. The colors were muted and earthy. But then, as I approached this mysterious place called Sedona, the scenery began to change. The soil turned first to a sandy mauve, and then to a rusty orange color. In the distance, I could see dramatic red sandstone buttes jutting upward into the crystal clear blue sky. A lush forest of deep green junipers and pines skirted these formations, contrasting and complementing their bright, ruddy hue.

As I experienced Sedona for the first time, I found myself in a state of overwhelming awe. They say that there are special vortexes of energy there, and, experiencing it that first time as I did, I believe it. It was like I was transported back to a simpler, more beautiful time and space. For the first time in many years, I felt like I could breathe. As I explored the canyons, the red rock formations seemed to become animated, living figures before my eyes—a standing Indian, a howling coyote, a group of boys laughing in the sun. I swore to myself at that moment, at the age of twenty-five, that I would retire there some day. Many decades later, I would make my dream a reality. For me and my friends from the LA playground, my new home of Sedona would become our place of retreat as we gathered to reunite and rejuvenate. Sedona proved to be a great place to shoot a round of golf, play a game of poker, and tell a few jokes and stories.

Then one day, like a lightning bolt from the clear blue sky, the news came that our beloved teammate Billy Consolo was gone. Receiving the news on the phone, I stood there incredulous, unable to take in the reality of it. Billy had always seemed like the strongest among us. He had not been sick, so there was no warning at all. This was the kid we called Superman. I had never known a more alive person in my life. How could he suddenly die like that, vanishing forever?

So, Sedona became our gathering place once again, but this time to mourn instead of to party. On that fall day, we had been up since well before sunrise. We made our way down the rocky terrain slowly, some struggling, toward a picturesque sandstone clearing with water-filled holes that reflected the image of nearby Cathedral Rock. This stunning setting was named Secret Mesa, but the secret of its splendor had been well-known for some time.

The Secret Mesa

When our age-toughened group of men reached the location with the best observation point, we spontaneously sat down and formed a circle on the hard sandstone, as if we were part of an ancient ritual that we instinctively understood. We were living through the most daunting, soul-searching stage of life known to man, known to the world as "old age." We tried to ignore our own dwindling lifespans while watching with trepidation as loved ones dropped around us. Some had their religious faith to fall back on, and others relied on their ability to take care of their bodies, hoping they could trick the reaper into staying away for a few more years.

The sun had fully risen, and its glowing rays lit the already dazzling background scenery. The men pulled out their cameras to get some rare early-morning shots to take home. The picturesque scene changed color and texture, becoming a totally different landscape as the sun and clouds moved along.

The largest of the men, Frank Layana, had traveled the farthest, from Thailand. He commented, "It's a beautiful spot, but, now that we're here, what are we going to do?" Being a religious man, there was some skepticism and maybe a little apprehension in his voice. Attending a spiritual service for a departed friend on a red rock in the middle of the Arizona high desert was an experience he had never expected in his lifetime.

I stood in the middle of the circle, acting as the host of this peculiar gathering. I quietly replied, "We're here to honor and celebrate the life of our beloved brother and teammate, Billy Consolo."

I glanced with quizzical eyes into the collective gaze of my teammates and received blank stares in return. My immediate thought was that maybe this type of memorial service wasn't such an appealing idea after all. A touch of awkward embarrassment was added to the already somber mood.

We had parked our two vans about three hundred yards away on the dirt road and had marched down the rock-strewn path to the mind-blowing view before us. Thus, it was too late to be troubled about their apparent apathy. Besides, whether any of us were able to admit it, we needed something to help us get a grip on the reality of this loss we had experienced. Losing Billy was like losing a stitch on the outside of a baseball. We had to do something to tie ourselves back together or we might unravel completely. If an unconventional spiritual ceremony was all I could think of, well, at least it was something.

I tried to keep it low-key since I knew the men were dangling off the edge of their emotional tolerance abilities and probably weren't prepared for what might be coming their way. I placed a picture of Billy on the sandstone where everyone could see it. This gathering was all about him and how we would proceed onward without our leader.

We had arrived from all over the West, Southwest, Texas, and even as far away as Thailand to unite the last ten members of a baseball team on which we had played over a half century ago.

We were in Sedona struggling to move forward following a death that had shocked all of us. William Angelo Consolo had died in his sleep from an unforeseen, sudden heart attack about seven months earlier. And although he expired quickly and painlessly—the way anyone would choose to go—the remainder of his teammates were devastated and traumatized by the sudden loss.

The hardest hit among us was, of course, Billy's best friend and confidant, George. To millions he had become known as Sparky Anderson, one of the most successful and famous managers in baseball history, but to us he was still just George or Georgie, the kid you could always count on in a scrap. He was like a boy vigilante on the playground. Cheaters and bullies beware!

Not so long ago, George had been so strong that you would swear his muscles were made out of steel wire. But today, rambling across the sandstone landscape, it looked like he had a hundred-pound weight on his back. He looked gaunt and tired, like a punch to the gut had taken the wind out of him for good.

"How dare he die on us without saying good-bye," someone muttered.

"How could he die on us without a parting joke?" someone responded.

Billy was the one among our group that none of us thought would ever die, especially at the relatively young age of seventy-three. He was the most gifted baseball player we had ever seen in the years we had grown up together playing in the parks and vacant lots of Los Angeles. His charisma was clearly evident, both on and off the baseball field. He was the glue that kept the team members together, the man who kept us laughing with his endless stories of his ten years playing and seventeen years coaching in the major leagues.

He told the same jokes every year that we were together, and every time we all laughed just as hard as the first time we had heard them. He delivered the same old walks-into-a-bar jokes as if we had never heard them before, rejuvenating them every time with his sheer enthusiasm. He told jokes the same way he lived his life—by inserting himself directly into everything he did.

• • • • • • • • • •

THE TEENAGED BILLY STOOD AT the end of the bench with one foot on the seat while leaning forward on the mitt propped on his knee. George stood slightly behind him, grinning with his arms crossed and a wide-footed stance. The rest of us seventeen-year-olds sat on the bench with eager expressions on our faces like choirboys waiting for communion. Finally, Billy blessed us with his offering.

"A pony walked into a bar and ordered a drink." He shifted a bit, pretending to get serious. A few of us snickered in anticipation. He continued, "The bartender said, 'What was that? I couldn't hear you.'" Billy cupped his hand around his ear to imitate the bartender. "And the pony said, 'Oh, sorry. I'm a little horse.'" With that, all the boys erupted in loud bellows of laughter. George laughed the loudest, smacked Billy on the back with his mitt, and said, "You and your dumb-ass jokes. C'mon, guys, get off your butts!" Heeding George's cue, we all got up from the bench and readied ourselves for baseball practice.

Billy Consolo was one of those good-natured, good-looking boys who are loved by kids and adults alike. He was slim but strong, with long and wiry arms and legs. His face was always friendly with a near-permanent grin and dark, sparkling eyes. He always dressed sharp and kept his dark brown hair neatly trimmed, which, combined with his magnetic personality, made him a favorite among the girls.

His best friend, George Anderson, might seem his opposite at first glance. Shorter than Billy, George's physique was not the typical athlete's, but he was nonetheless muscular and strong. His head seemed to be just a little bit too big for his body, and his big brown eyes could stare right through you if you crossed him. His two ears popped out like tea cups from the sides of his head, giving him the appearance of a guard dog on constant alert. A shag of light brown hairs grew straight up from the top of his head, defying all attempts to lay them flat.

On the baseball field, these two boys worked like one machine. Billy was a natural athlete who could simply do anything, and George was the kind of athlete who would always go one step further than you thought he could. Together, they added up to everything you could ever ask for in teammates in terms of great baseball play.

Baseball was everything to us in those days. When you are a kid, life is still an abstract concept because it has yet to be lived. That, for any kid, can be a scary proposition. There are so many questions that linger in the back of the mind at seventeen: Will I make it? Will I succeed? What will life hold for me? Yet the game of baseball was there for us, teaching us in its symbolic terms what life was all about. It taught us how to win and how to lose. Baseball taught us to shake off life's errors and to embrace success as well as failure. It taught us that each at bat is a whole new start. Each new pitch was like a new day. You never knew what life would pitch at you. That ball of life comes at you looking like a blur with a split second to decide to swing or not. Focusing on a speeding ball was like figuring out life and if it had thrown you a curve.

Swinging feebly for a single wasn't in our DNA; we wanted the long ball out of life. Languishing on first base wasn't acceptable; we wanted to get home and quickly. Hitting, as in life, was not about half swings but full-body all-out efforts that sounded loud and pure when wood connected solidly with leather. Striking out was also a byproduct of swinging for the fences, but we didn't care. Three strikes was the price you willingly paid for the lottery chance of "hitting one out." Early on we were taught to never be *called out on strikes; always go down swinging*. Failure was a big part of baseball and of life, and the earlier you learned that the better.

Baseball taught us to always take responsibility for our errors and admit, "I really screwed up *that* play" and then go on playing it like it never happened. It also taught us that every man on the field matters and that your teammates will always be there to cheer for you when you make it back home again.

Hollywood, circa 1939: My mother, two sisters, and me.

2

Fallen Angels

Today, when people think of Los Angeles, they think of it as a city without a history, perhaps because it does not have its roots in the English colonies like Boston, New York, and other East Coast cities. But in reality, it is a very old city, originally founded as Pueblo de Los Angeles in 1781. In its infancy, the city was planned and governed as a colony of Spain, and this cultural influence helped to create its original charm through Spanish architecture and colorful places like Olvera Street in downtown LA. For most of its history, Los Angeles had been a delightful *paradiso* by the sea.

But by 1942, the City of Angels had begun to lose its celestial wings. In the previous decade, the population had gained more than a million people, most of them expecting the lifestyle they had seen in newsreels and Hollywood films. Industrial plants of various forms had taken root, slowly but surely replacing the agriculture that had previously dominated the economic landscape. The automotive industry was especially prominent, and it had successfully instilled the notion that every functional adult in LA should have their own set of wheels as their primary mode of transportation. What little mass transit existed languished under the effects of the LA car culture as politicians sold out the needs of the city populace to oil and automotive special-interest groups.

The once-charming little city was spreading in every direction with a bumper crop of cheap, mass-construction houses built on the same land that formerly sprouted plants to eat or to replant in home gardens. Soon the roads of LA were clogged with traffic as people made their way to work from the expanding suburban areas. The Arroyo Seco Parkway, the first freeway in the Western United States, had been completed in 1940, connecting Pasadena and downtown LA, but that offered little help to most commuters. A byproduct of all this "progress" was smog, which now stained the formerly unblemished blue sky with layers of ugly brown haze. On the worst days, visibility was less than two city blocks and some people even donned gas masks to relieve their burning eyes and lungs.

On top of all this rapid change, the citizens of Los Angeles were dealing with the effects of war. The Japanese attack on Pearl Harbor had occurred in December of the previous year, marking the United States' entry into WWII. Of course, this event shocked the country as a whole, but it hit, both literally and figuratively, closer to home for Los Angelinos. The anxiety even spawned an air raid that turned out to be a false alarm triggered by a wayward weather balloon, later facetiously referred to as The Battle of Los Angeles. On top of that, the War's appetite for aircraft and other implements of war fueled LA's already rapidly growing industrialism.

For me, only a small boy of seven at the time, all of these changes were a mere shadow in the background of my consciousness. Yes, I would notice the worry on grown-up faces, and I could feel the burn in my young lungs on the smoggy days, but for me life was still a carefree adventure of play and mischief-making. My best friend was Kelly Moffit, my brother-in-arms in the only war we cared about—the war between our need for wild amusements and the forces that sought to civilize us. We had been inseparable the last four years that we lived in the neighborhood together, and we were notorious on our street for engineering creative hijinks. When neighbors saw us coming down the street together, they would proclaim, "Uh oh! Here comes double trouble."

Kelly was a towhead, and I had dark curly hair. Although we were opposite in appearance, our devious little minds were always on the same page. Our philosophy was simple: Life was more fun when rules were broken and chaos abounded. If one of us didn't think of the perfect act of disruption to fit a given occasion, the other would. We were full of wildly inventive ideas that most kids our age never dared to dream about.

One time, we decided to parachute off the roof of my house. In our childish minds, we actually believed that bed sheets would be suitable to allow us to float down slowly and safely, like the paratroopers we had seen in newsreels. So, we held the corners of the sheets in our clenched fists and took a flying leap. This resulted in a bump on the head for Kelly and a sore, swollen butt for me. In this case, we were our own victims, but more often than not, someone else bore the brunt of our ill-conceived shenanigans. Whenever we would disturb the neighbors with one of our silly plans, Kelly's parents would insinuate that I was the instigator and leader and that Kelly was a mere follower. But actually there was no leader. We were a duo who fed hungrily off each other's zany ideas.

Kelly's parents were transplants from the Midwest. They were body builders and sun worshipers who had swapped a routine parking space back east for the fast lane in Hollywood. Kelly's mom and dad were typical of the many people who had come to California seeking to revamp their boring lives with the glitz and glamour of Hollywood. After gaining jobs in the movie industry, they were reveling in it. They were a good-looking couple who would sun bathe in skimpy swimsuits and pump iron in their backyard when free time was available. Kelly was the apple of their eyes, and he could do no wrong.

Naturally, we were fascinated with taboo substances, especially the sort that emanated from our own bodies. We soon began the curious habit of collecting our own urine in empty bottles and jars. We became connoisseurs of a sort, developing pride in our growing collection. After all, why should one waste such a beautiful thing by flushing it down the toilet? Instead we relished in watching it squirt out of our penises (another favorite object of obsession) into a glass containment device, where it would sit, warm and frothy, awaiting our future attentions.

At first, we simply admired our collection, holding it up to the sun to admire its yellow hue and comparing our respective production capabilities. When the initial fascination began to where off, we knew we had to find some other use for our collection. It had to be shared with the world in some way. It was just too good of a medium to be wasted. So, being the mischief artists that we were, we came up with the ultimate plan—Operation Pee Bomb.

Nimbly holding a jar in one hand, we both climbed up an old oak that provided a canopy over the sidewalk. Balancing ourselves on a thick branch that jutted out over the sidewalk, we were conveniently camouflaged by a thick curtain of green oak leaves. Commencing with our plan, we unscrewed the lids of our jars, being careful to avoid splashing any of the contents on ourselves. Then we both recoiled back and scrunched up our faces, disgusted and delighted by the smell. "Ripe!" I said with glee, noting the especially potent nature of the aged brew. Kelly nodded and we both giggled, almost giving ourselves away. "Shhhhh!" I implored as footsteps were heard coming down the sidewalk toward the tree. We focused and readied ourselves for attack. The enemy was in view—my sister Mary Lee, who was three years older than me.

When she was squarely under our perch, we let our cargo go. "Bombs away!" we yelled. The stream of stinky yellow pee landed smack on the top of her head and shoulders. Standing for a few seconds in shock, she then realized exactly what had hit her. Her clothes were completely drenched. She began to scream and didn't stop screaming as she ran toward home. Wanting to witness the mayhem, I followed her home, even though I knew I was going to get it for sure. I delighted at the sight of my sister peeling off her pee-soaked clothes on the way to the bath as she screamed, "I'll never be clean again!" After her bath, she glared angrily at me as she slammed the clothes down into the trash. It was all I could do to hold in my giggles.

Needless to say we got into big-time trouble for that stupid choice of a target, but trouble was our middle name, so why should we care? We had been before the tribunal many times, and we knew the caper would blow over and that whatever punishment we received would be worth the entertainment value. We were more than willing to accept the reprimand and short-term probation as payment for yet another accomplishment to be logged into our personal naughtiness hall of fame. We were literally full of piss and vinegar that earned us our reputation as cute little boys with sick little minds, and we didn't mind at all.

Then, in 1942 when so much around us was also changing, our dirty dynamic duo was forced to end. My parents decided it was time to move to a new neighborhood. I watched with tear-filled eyes as the moving van, filled with all our household belongings, pulled away from the curb in front of our empty duplex unit on North Havenhurst Drive. My family was moving from the only home I had known since we moved to Hollywood in 1937. We had moved there from El Centro, California, where my father was in the produce business. His job with the family business took him from that little farming community to the big city of LA about 250 miles northwest. Since I was only three years old when we moved to Hollywood, it was the only home that I remembered living in in my young life.

On that fateful day, Kelly sat beside me on the curb as we cried our eyes out. As our tears fell into the gutter, my mother walked up to us holding the keys to our car and asked, "What are you boys up to now? Why are you crying?"

I put on a convincing show of opposition and defiance for my mother's benefit. She always had an abundance of patience with me when I resisted her, but this day was different and she was not in the mood to debate the subject.

"Mom, I don't want to move. I love it here, and I don't want to leave my friend Kelly."

She tried to console me. "I know it's hard to leave your friends, but we're only moving about twenty minutes from here. You can hop on a bus and be here to visit Kelly in no time at all."

She was right. During the early 1940s, buses and streetcars ran all over the Los Angeles area, and even at our young age we were allowed to take advantage of the efficient transportation system. That wasn't good enough for me, though.

"I don't want to be twenty minutes away from Kelly! It's too far, and besides, we have important things to do!"

The "important things" were, of course, the mischievous deeds that struck alarm in the hearts of our neighbors. With me leaving the neighborhood, there would be a collective sigh of relief from the neighbors. Without Kelly and me working together as a team, our street was bound to become tragically tranquil. How dare my parents subject the neighborhood to such unbridled quietude?

My mother was a gentle, intelligent woman, tall and slim with wavy hair and beautiful blue eyes. She possessed the figure and looks of a model but only yearned to be a mother to her three children. She had her own problems with this move; she was leaving cherished neighbors that were also irreplaceable friends.

She was saying good-bye to our next door neighbors, the Glenn family, who were the best neighbors you could ever want in a lifetime. Auntie Glenn was a grandmother type who treated my sisters and me as she would her own family. We lovingly identified her as Auntie, which was a name of endearment she had earned through her loving demeanor. It was disrespectful in the

Italian culture for children to refer to elders by their first name; in fact we never knew her first name. We just called her Auntie Glenn, and we loved her like one!

Although there was a driveway separating our two side doors, it was as though our homes were connected. We would trek between the two homes, without knocking, as though they were one. My sisters and I would receive soothing back rubs almost on a daily basis from Auntie Glenn. Undoubtedly we would miss her and the other wonderful neighbors. It was a village where people ambled from one home to another. No one locked their doors or feared any type of crime.

This move had fallen directly onto my mother's shoulders, and she wasn't looking forward to the extra work and stress. She had three active children to care for, and this move would add to her already difficult job. It wasn't good timing on my part to pick this particular time to be a childish nuisance.

"Come on, Carlie. We must be at the new house when the moving van gets there, and they have a head start on us." She waved her hand toward our car parked in the driveway, but I didn't move. She was finished trying to placate me. "Get moving! Say good-bye to Kelly. We're leaving now!"

I sulked and whined my way to the car where my two sisters had been waiting for us. I gave Kelly a long hug, and we vowed to be friends forever. We pulled away from our vacated home, heading south on Havenhurst. I looked out the rear window of the car, watching Kelly waving and wiping the tears from his eyes. I cried and moaned all the way to the new house, telling my mother and sisters that I would never like it there.

As we approached our new home on Olmsted Avenue, the moving van was waiting for us, and I continued ranting. "I don't know anyone here, and I bet there are no kids on this block! Besides, I'll never find another friend like Kelly!" Actually, that would be an extraordinary blessing for the sanity of the new neighborhood.

I pleaded my case to an empty jury box as everybody was struggling with their own emotions concerning the move. Even my two sisters were on the fence about the relocation. We all would miss those frequent back rubs from Auntie Glenn and the family-oriented neighborhood that we were leaving behind. However, like it or not, we were relocating our residence the short eight-mile distance from Hollywood to Los Angeles.

Carl, 8, and his younger sister, Phyllis Jean

Joltin' Joe DiMaggio in his 1941 hitting streak of fifty-six games

3

Land of Milk and Honey

IN MY YOUNG MIND, JOLTIN' Joe DiMaggio was the man who had it all. Throughout my childhood in the 1940s he was the unstoppable Yankee Clipper with the unbeatable hitting streak of fifty-six games in 1941. Even after he retired in 1951, his legend loomed large as one of the great superheroes of baseball. Looking at him, he seemed to be little more than a lanky, awkward-looking guy. But when he swung the bat, he swung with a grace and power that seemed to exemplify all that was good and right with the world. To top it all off, this icon of baseball married the ultimate icon of Hollywood glamour, Marilyn Monroe. Sure, they divorced a few years later, but we all knew he was the only one she ever really loved. He was the regular guy who had proven his strength, prowess, and agility, and every guy wanted to be him.

For most kids, dreaming of being Joe DiMaggio was nothing more than a daydream fantasy. For me, the dreams were further kindled by reality. After all, I had a lot in common with him. I shared Italian heritage and a last name with the man. My family name had indeed been DiMaggio until the process of Anglicization shortened it to Maggio. I didn't know this until much later in life. We even had the same middle name—him the Italian Paulo and me the English Paul. I, like him, was also the second-generation son of an Italian immigrant. It was not too hard for me to imagine that I was descended from the same royal baseball lineage as he. My uncle, who was also named Joe, fed my imaginings by making comparisons between Joltin' Joe's traits and mannerisms and those of my father and his siblings, the Maggio brothers. Stockpiling these facts in my brain, I dreamed of hitting balls out of the park and breaking records just like he had. They say that all we DiMaggios are related in some way or another, and I was willing to embrace the lineage.

Perhaps my baseball fantasy was a pipe dream, but dreams had made my family what it was, and dreams were still the main currency moving the country forward in my early years. My grandfather and grandmother had come to the United States from Sicily in 1918, dreaming of a better life in America, as so many others were at the time. They came in through Boston Harbor, one of those countless faces that you now see in old photographs of men and women unloading onto the pier like sardines from a trawler. If you look closely at those photographs, though, you can see the faint light of hope, along with a dash of bewilderment, in the eyes of every face turned toward the camera. I'm certain that my grandparents had the same light in their eyes, and I'm sure it was that light that led my family forward toward the American dream.

My father had followed his large family to America docking at Ellis Island a few years later in 1920 at the age of twenty-two. He had completed his time fighting for the Italian army against the Germans during World War I, and it was time for him to make a life of his own. The family at first settled in Weirton, West Virginia. Then in 1925, after hearing about California's bountiful sunshine and business opportunities, the Maggios heard the siren's call and headed west.

Southern California was a natural fit for my family since its Mediterranean climate matched the balmy weather of Sicily perfectly and even the Spanish architecture alluded to home. In the previous century, people had pointed to the hills of California and said, "There's gold in them there hills." But by the 1920s that gold was all but tapped out, and people were pointing to the fertile valleys below. A family friend had already struck it rich in the produce industry, and my family decided to follow suit.

Millions of years of ice age glacial progression had deposited layers of rich soil in flat, farm-ready layers in the California central and southern valleys. Combined with the mild weather and endless sunshine, California was now considered to be an agricultural cornucopia, supplying a wide variety of fruits, vegetables, and nuts to the entire nation and much of the world, as it still does today. At the time, most of the land outside of LA was covered with miles and miles of endless row crops and orange groves.

When my father arrived in the States, his brothers had an established business, so he had a job waiting for him. My father had an education equivalent to about the eighth grade in the US. While he learned English fairly well, he still had a slight Italian accent that would stick with him his entire life. My father and his seven brothers were the muscles that made the produce business a viable means of support for our family. Rising well before the crack of dawn, they would travel to the wholesale produce packing shed in the remote town of El Centro. They loaded delivery trucks with produce trucked from the Los Angeles produce market the night before. They would drive all over the southern portion of Imperial Valley, filling orders and taking new orders for the many markets in the area.

For me, however, life was idyllic and easy compared to that of my hardworking father. Los Angeles was a beautiful place to grow up in back in the day, not the congested megalopolis it is today. Although people were moving in fast from all parts of the country, there were still lots of open spaces and orange trees to separate the suburban areas from the downtown smog and traffic. I would cringe to watch housing pop up and people moving in, hoping vainly that the influx would eventually end and my paradise would be preserved. Somehow, everyone who moved in hoped that they would be the last, but it was never to be so.

While Southern California boasted agrarian bounty and beauty, it also crackled with electric excitement, thanks in large part to the Hollywood movie industry. Newsreels shown in movie theaters would advertise California sunshine along with all the tinsel town glamour, which seemed to draw even more people westward. Newspaper pictures of the Rose Parade also did their part, supporting the false notion that rain never fell in Southern California. Apocryphal tales about starlets being discovered in drugstores made people think they, too, could be a star. They moved in thinking they would be rubbing elbows with the stars, only to find that they were rubbing elbows with more and more disappointed people just like themselves.

Nevertheless, Los Angeles in the 1940s and ’50s was still my boyhood field of dreams. In those days, there was plenty of open space to explore and play ball in. A kid could get around on a functioning rapid transit system that had not yet succumbed to political power of the burgeoning auto industry. And we always felt safe—safe to leave the doors unlocked, to hitchhike to the next town, or to leave our bikes unattended. We were free to be kids in ways that kids now cannot enjoy.

As far as baseball was concerned, there were no major league teams in Southern California at the time—the Dodgers were still in Brooklyn and the Angels were still in their minor league embryonic state. Yet, baseball was still a favorite pastime and every boy’s fondest dream. In spite of the lack of major league ball, baseball talent grew here as well as oranges and onions. “It must be something in the water,” people would say. Maybe so, but it was more likely the year-round sunshine that allowed year-round baseball.

Just like movies and produce, we shipped off a yearly crop of talent to the world of baseball.

My family moved to an area called Leimert Park, about eight miles south of Hollywood. In 1927, developer Walter H. Leimert purchased 231 acres of bean fields twenty minutes west of downtown Los Angeles for two million dollars. Leimert envisioned growth and industrialization as large eastern manufacturing companies were looking at the West Coast as a place to set up satellite facilities. Leimert Park was to be a "workplace dwelling" project. The development was to provide all the elements required for upscale living at affordable prices. At the time, it was one of the first planned communities of the type that would soon blanket greater Los Angeles and neighboring Orange County. It was designed to be a self-contained community with schools and shopping areas. So my parents bought a cookie-cutter three-bedroom, one-and-a-half-bath row house with a small back yard for around $7,500.

My mother, Lena, ran the house, as women of her generation were bound to do, with gentleness and strength. She was also of Italian heritage, a second-generation Sicilian born in Chicago on March 29, 1910, both parents having emigrated from Sicily in the early 1900s. She was educated in the States, graduating from Brawley Union High School in a quaint farming area of Southern California. In addition to her duties as housewife and mother, she proved herself to be quite a real estate maven. She read that section of the paper every day, checking all the new listings. Whenever she saved up enough money, she would buy small commercial buildings. A superb money manager, she accumulated a fair amount of property over the years. My father joked that she squeezed money so tightly and was so frugal that she made the buffalo on the nickel squeal. She was a totally Americanized entrepreneur, while my father was a newbie from the old country. What a pair!

My sister Mary Lee has always contended that their relationship was similar to Desi and Lucy in the popular TV sitcom *I*

Love Lucy. He had an Italian accent and flawed English, and she possessed natural comic timing. She could mimic his Italian accent to perfection, and even he would laugh. Sometimes she wasn't trying to be funny, yet it always came out that way. We kids would be rolling on the floor trying not to laugh. She never understood what was so hilarious, never realizing that her commentaries were so funny!

My dad was bald, so he loved to wear hats and had a wide collection. One day he came home from shopping wearing a swanky straw hat of Maurice Chevalier vintage. I thought he looked spiffy and so did he, so he pranced around the house showing off his stylish new headpiece. My mother had a strange phobia about straw hats; it probably was the result of having grown up in a farming community. She didn't consider them worthy to be considered even low fashion. She actually thought that only farmers wore them. To her, it was like wearing a sign that read *cafone,* a derogatory Italian word referring to an uneducated, uncouth person. She let her opinion be known without holding back her feelings. "Paul, you look like a damn buffoon in that hat. Take it back to the store. It's making me sick."

He ignored her comments and continued to sashay around the house, doing some soft shoe dancing while twirling the straw chapeau. He tried his best to convince my mother that she should accept the hat because it brought class to his persona.

"Don't you think it looks dapper?" he inquired of my mother.

"Dapper? More like daffy," she retorted.

"Aw, come on. You'll be the envy of all the ladies with me by your side."

But she wasn't buying anything to do with the straw top and wouldn't let up on her sustained barrage of nonstop hat insults. She stood there with her arms crossed as he floated around the room. "Dumb! Let's call it a dunce cap," she quipped.

Finally, he relented, "Okay, okay. I get the picture. I'll take it back tomorrow! Now, *statte zitte*!" (That means "be quiet!" in Sicilian.)

She wasn't nearly finished harassing him over that straw hat. She prolonged her rant with innuendoes that challenged his sanity and fashion sense. Building herself into a state of Italian fury, she let out her tirade, cutting him right to the bone.

"I work to make this house decent, and then you come home having bought this stupid thing! Lord, deliver me from this demon in my husband!" She was overreacting and didn't know when to let well enough alone. She should have stopped her outburst when he said he would take it back, but she didn't.

He didn't say a word. He looked her straight in the eye, took off the hat, held it in his outstretched hands for a second, and then let it drop to the floor. He stood over the hat, looking down at it with a smile, and then proceeded to step on top of it. My mother's eyes opened wide, and she started to protest his weirdness. I'm sure she was upset that the expensive hat was being sacrificed because of her. But my dad put his index finger up to his smiling lips. Then he started to do a little tarantella dance on the hat with his hands on his hips. Then he changed the mood as though he was imitating a smooth dance step from a Fred Astaire movie. He moved with perfect, gliding precision over the kitchen floor as the hat shuffled along between his feet. He manipulated it like a soccer player attempting to score a goal. He then jumped up, clicked his heels together, and came down squarely on top of the straw hat. His dance slowly transformed into the monster stomp as he trampled it to smithereens, until there was nothing left but tiny bits of straw all over the kitchen. He did it with absolute grace, without a hint of violence throughout the entire routine.

We three children were dumbfounded, waiting to see what type of activity would transpire in this fast moving melodrama now that the hat was just bits and pieces. Nothing happened; the incident was over!

My father excused himself by saying, "I've got to make a phone call."

They mutually retreated into silence when they both realized each had slipped into childish behavior in front of their kids. My mother stood there wide-eyed with her mouth open and never said another word.

I looked at my sisters as if to say, "What the heck just happened?" They just shrugged their shoulders.

My older sister, Mary Lee, swept up the remnants of what was left of the hat, trying hard to restrain her impulse to burst out laughing. Neither of my parents ever mentioned that straw hat incident again. It was like it never occurred.

Carl, 7, with older sister, Mary Lee, 10

Transfiguration Catholic school, sixth grade, 1946

4

Impure Thought Control

Although there was a public school only half of a block away, I attended a Catholic school six blocks from our new home in Leimert Park. In retrospect, I don't think I got a better education at the Catholic middle school than my friends did in the public school system. Perhaps my parents didn't know what else to do about our spiritual education than to let the nuns do their best to save our sinful souls while simultaneously instilling grammar and multiplication tables. The nuns who taught at our grammar school were hardly a fun-loving bunch, and they transformed learning into a dreaded chore burdened by the constant specter of reprimand and punishment. I can't count how many times I was sent to the principal's office for doing absolutely nothing wrong.

Our playground at Transfiguration Catholic Grammar School on Santa Barbara Avenue had a yellow line painted down the middle of the yard. The boys played on one half, and the girls played on the other. God forbid that they should play together and learn to interact in healthy concert.

The nuns, or perhaps the policymaking clergy, seemed to think that boys and girls playing together stimulated "impure thoughts" that led inevitably to mortal sin. This notion seemed a little far-fetched to me. But the yellow line was not an imaginary line that could be crossed without consequence. Serious ramifications awaited those who were caught on the wrong side of the line.

One morning before school started, I was playing baseball on the boys' side of the line. The ball was hit toward me, flying over my head and over the yellow line into the forbidden land of femininity. It was definitely a homerun!

In the fourth grade I had no interest in girls whatsoever. I had two annoying female antagonists (i.e., sisters) at home, and my whole life was overstocked with schoolgirls. The last thing on my mind as I traversed the banned side of the schoolyard was the possibility of chatting with any girls.

As I trotted across the Mason-Dixon Line into the banned territory, I was surprised to find that not a single impure thought had entered my mind. At the time, I wasn't sure if I had ever had a genuinely impure thought. I suppose I had tried to have a couple at that age, but I had never succeeded at having a real, full-blown one. If the nuns hadn't harped, "All impure thoughts are a mortal sin, and you will go straight to hell for thinking it," I probably wouldn't have even tried to think of one. But I figured there must be something worthwhile in them since they caused such a fuss. Since the nuns were responsible for putting the intriguing concept of impure thoughts in my mind, I wondered if they were the ones to blame for my curiosity! Besides I never knew what the punishment was for breaking the rule, what could they do to me? Hang me?

Trying to ignore the potential consequences, I chased the baseball into the girls' section to retrieve it. As I spotted the brazen baseball lying under the girls' lunch bench with no one near it, I thought, "Oh, good. This is going to be easy. No one will even notice me."

On my knees, I reached under the bench to pick up the

naughty ball; I suddenly felt the aura of authority hovering over me. I glanced over to see a familiar pair of black high-top shoes appear and I instantly knew who was standing in them. Garbed in the customary black and white costume, Sister Mary Margarita glared at me through her thick bifocals. As far as she was concerned, either God himself had reassigned my gender or I would face immediate perdition for being on the girls' side of the playground.

"You know you're not supposed to be over here! What are you doing here?" she demanded with a distinct hint of hate glinting from her squinty eyes.

"Getting our baseball that was hit over here!" I said, still on my knees, showing no remorse and holding the baseball in my hand as irrefutable evidence.

"No! You're over here to talk to the girls, aren't you?"

I stood there looking at her in speechless disbelief.

"Aren't you?" she said louder.

"No! No, Sister Mary Moustache ... um, I mean Sister Mary Margarita." We kids had christened her with that name because of the dark fuzz growing on her upper lip. In my stressed condition, I had let it slip. I was sunk for sure.

I put on a nice show of tenacity, but now I was getting nervous. I had seen this kind of "nunish" conduct before from Sister Mary Margarita. She was torturously anti-male and never missed an opportunity to show her bias. She took all her frustrations out on boys, watching like a hawk for a chance to sink her talons into those committing minor infractions and then proudly hauling her prey off to the principal's office.

She was infamous for barging into the boy's bathroom when it was full of urinating schoolboys. If they were talking or having too much fun, she would grab the back of their shirt collar and yank them away from the urinal while they were still in full stream. She seemed to take perverse pleasure in watching young boys pee all over the floor and on themselves. So I knew I was in for a rough ride with this notorious nun zeroing in on me. I tried to defend myself, but I knew it was pointless.

"I'm here to get the ..."

She interrupted emphatically, "NO YOU ARE NOT! You're here to talk to the girls! You like talking to the girls."

By this time there was a small crowd of female students surrounding us and gawking at me like I was an extraterrestrial being who had just been dropped into their yard from a spaceship. They knew who I was, but they acted like it was the first time they had ever seen me. Fear of guilt by association had taken hold of their minds.

She grabbed my arm and started pulling me toward the school door. I didn't resist because I knew from experience that these situations were like quicksand. Resistance would only get me in deeper. I had learned to let the nuns play out their devious little design. If I played my cards right, maybe it would be over soon.

"Come with me! We're having a talk with Sister Marcella!"

Sister Marcella was the head honcho of the school. She was the one penguin who could peck you to bits. No one wanted to deal with her. She never missed a chance to de-masculinize a boy or de-feminize a girl. Her lot in life was to neuter our psyches so that our thoughts would be forever asexual. Prepubescent intervention before adolescence hit, I suppose. Yet, when speaking with Father Murphy, she would giggle like a hyena in heat. I often wondered what was going on in Sister Marcella's brain, in terms of impure thoughts, when she was talking to Father Murphy.

Sister Mary Margarita dragged me through the play yard and into the principal's office. I was in familiar surroundings, as I had been there many times before, mostly on trumped-up charges. As she pushed me through the office door, she squealed, "He was over in the girls' yard talking to them!" I tried to fight back. "I wasn't talking to anybody. I was getting our baseball that had gone over there."

An ominous smile appeared on Sister Marcella's face. She

"Why didn't you just tell us that you wanted to play in the girls' yard? We can arrange it so you will fit in with a uniform."
—Sister Marcella

lived for situations like these. I could see the wheels in her head spinning as she concocted a scheme.

She purred, "Oh, I get it. You want to play with the girls. Well, we can arrange that."

She pointed to the other penguin, "Go get me a uniform that will fit him, a girl's uniform." Her face gleamed with pride as she reflected upon her masterful plan. For good reason, she was renowned for her unique style of cruel, punitive justice.

"Why didn't you just tell us that you wanted to play in the girls' yard? We'll find you a uniform so you can fit in."

When the girls' uniform arrived, I was instructed to put it on over my clothes and roll up my pant legs to expose my bare legs.

"She needs a hat. Get her a hat to go with her outfit."

Smitten with her own instantaneous, creative imagination, she was getting more inventive by the minute. I, on the other hand, felt a heavy blanket of shame and humiliation cover over me. But I had been taught through my Italian upbringing to respect my elders, so I did what I was told. Like any good Catholic schoolboy, I went through the motions of respecting them, while inside I secretly loathed them.

She placed the hat on my head and announced, "There! Now you're ready to play with the girls."

Finally, it had gone too far. I had to plead my case. "Sister, this isn't fair. I didn't do anything wrong! Can I take this dress off now?"

She had a ready answer. "Now, you don't think we dressed you up in this uniform just for our own amusement, do you? No, we want the whole school to see what happens when the rules are broken."

"But I didn't talk to anyone. Honest! I won't do it again!" I appealed, near tears.

Sister Marcella loved it when boys begged for mercy. "You bet you won't do it again!" she quipped.

Morning playtime was over, and now the whole school assembled on the playground to recite the Pledge of Allegiance. I was scheduled to be their showcased "disciplinary model" for the morning. I suppose this was their sadistic way of keeping everyone scared and obedient, a little bit like the public beheadings of medieval times. The bell rang and all eight classes assembled for the show to begin.

As Sister Marcella marched out to lead the pledge, I was right behind her dressed in my new "outfit," hat and all. I stood in the very middle of the assembly, looking pretty but feeling embarrassed and stupid. But I was going along for the ride; I had no other option! It was their show, and I was the stooge in their little farce.

I had seen many other boys put in similar positions before, so I was not afraid of being made an example. However, no boy had ever before been forced to wear a girl's uniform. My intention was to take all they could dish out and come out unscathed with a smile on my face.

Sister Marcella pointed toward me and announced to a laughing assembly, "I would like to introduce our new girl in school. Her name is Carla, and she wants to play in the girls' yard!"

To show the rebellious side of my personality, I waved with a semi-disguised, middle-finger salute to the giggling assembly, smiling all the while. No one noticed my brief obscenity, except a few of the boys in my class.

The boys in my grade played along by flirting with me and asking for a date. "Hey, Carla! You're so cute! How about a date?" One kid made smooching sounds to really get at me. Everyone got a huge laugh at my expense and no one laughed harder than the nuns. All the boys cringed a bit inside, though, knowing that at any given time during the school year, they could be standing in my shoes as the butt of the nuns' comic exemplum.

Looking back at these nuns' exploits, I really have to wonder what their real motivations were. When initiated into the convent, these women had taken a vow to be "Christ-like" in their daily lives. Even then I wondered, "Would Christ have taken part in a degrading display like that?" It seemed to me this was everything Jesus preached against!

Even though I played along that day and did my best to keep smiling, something inside of me felt deeply disappointed. I had wanted to learn something deeper from these people who were supposed to be God's representatives. I had wished they would help us find answers about the big questions in life: Why am I here? Why do people die? How am I supposed to live well and be happy? Instead, all I learned about was humiliation and shame. Yet, a fighting spirit inside of me knew that there must be something more to life.

I guessed I would have to learn it some other way and in some other place.

What was it about playing and hitting a baseball that was transforming my life for the better? It seemed like playing baseball and being a part of a team crushed my phobia toward girls.

5

Exorcising the Demons

Within three months of moving to the new neighborhood that I had vowed to hate, I discovered the park of my dreams that would become my second home and a large part of a new lifestyle.

I was riding my bike in the vicinity of Dorsey High School when I happened upon a large, grassy open area. As I pedaled closer, the celestial vista opened up like I was looking through a wide angle lens camera. Green grass lay before me like an endless carpet that contrasted beautifully against the blue sky. Suddenly, I felt all the burden and sadness of moving had been lifted off my shoulders. I could feel my chest expand as I inhaled deeply. As I exhaled, the word *wow* slowly and involuntarily passed over my lips with my breath. I was full of awe and amazed, truly mesmerized, by the scene in front of me. In the distance, I could see boys hitting and catching balls. I might as well have been entering a grand cathedral in Europe.

Riding onto the deep green grass, I was delighted to encounter this blissful multisport sanctuary that was only a short bike ride from my new home. Rancho La Cienega Playground was akin to discovering a pearl in a peanut butter jar. It was one of the top playgrounds in Southern California, and it was a mile directly west of my brand new residence.

For me, it was love at first sight. I couldn't believe that it had a baseball diamond on each corner of its ten acres. It also had four tennis courts and numerous basketball backboards. I loved participating in all sports, and this was an athlete's ultimate paradise.

Various sports proceeded in full motion as I walked through the complex. My first instinct was to get a bat and ball and join in on the fun. I loved the kinetic energy the place radiated, and I began to visualize myself functioning within this exciting environment. It was my kind of summer space.

As I began to frequent the playground on a daily basis and became acquainted with new friends, I felt more and more at home and wasn't thinking about Hollywood or Kelly Moffit very often. I had found a young boy's Nirvana, and it would quickly eclipse the last four years' worth of Hollywood memories.

I had swiftly created two new major obsessions—baseball and the perfect place to play it. To hell with Hollywood; that part of my past was history! My plans to get on a bus to visit Kelly somehow faded from my mind, so he must have found some way to exist without me. I did see Kelly a few times over the years, but the relationship never thrived without the Havenhurst Drive connection. Now a couple years older, it was like we had never known each other, and we had nothing to say to each other.

The playground director at Rancho was Benny Lefebvre, a short, muscular man with a broad smile. He might as well have been the king of our boyhood world, and we hung on his every word as though it came from a sage. Benny knew exactly when to say something and when to stay quiet. He knew when a kid needed direction and when it was best to let him figure things out on his own. He was very friendly and helpful to me, the new kid on his playground, and he nurtured my budding fascination with baseball. Benny had the personality of a diplomat who made everyone he met feel special. He didn't care who you were or how great an athlete you were. He treated everyone the same.

I remember meeting Benny while still a young elementary school kid. I could tell he was the guy with whom to talk to get in on the games, but I was shy. I said sheepishly, "Uh … sir?" Benny turned around and smiled down at me.

"Hey, big guy. Wanna play some ball?" he asked.

"Sure!" I said, beaming. "How do I get on a team?"

"Just show up, kid," he responded. He was hitting ground balls to two guys in the field. I could already see who the star was. Billy was scooping up the balls with absolute deftness, while George was just learning. Billy was smooth and well-coordinated; he made fielding ground balls look easy. On the other hand George struggled with the whole process of catching a ball and also with his temper. When he missed a ball he would throw his mitt at the ball like it was the ball's fault. Benny paused and called Billy and George off the field and introduced me to them. As we shook hands I felt a strong bonding friendship overtake me. These two guys were going to be friends forever.

Benny organized the baseball summer league teams that at the time were called Midget Leagues—there was no political correctness in those days—which evolved much later into Little League Baseball. During the winter months, there was a football league in which we could display our macho male skills. If you didn't want to play on a team, there were always the handball courts, basketball hoops, and just about anything else you could imagine. Boys could take their choice of a seemingly infinite array of activities. The playground was a mega sports department store for addicted athletes to peruse and enjoy all summer. There was never a stationary moment. The place was constantly buzzing with action and people in motion. It stimulated my senses beyond anything I had ever experienced!

Baseball on the playground was the sport of choice for most of us because size didn't matter as much as in the other sports.

There was a pick-up game in progress at all times on each of the baseball diamonds at all four corners of the playground. I loved to play all three major sports, but baseball was my favorite one of all. Just like Joltin' Joe, I was totally hooked on the game and would remain a hardcore addict my whole life.

I soon discovered that hitting a baseball and running the bases exorcized the demons in my head that had accrued under the influence of my religious background. I was exercising my body and exorcizing my mind at the same time. Through this magnificent sport, I was gaining confidence and starting to get some insight into what I was all about.

We would congregate at *Rancho,* as we called it, throughout the year, whether during the long days of summer or the short days of winter. We had a smorgasbord of sports made available to us. Baseball ruled the playground almost year-round. We would use the old hands-up-the-bat routine to decide who got first dibs on Billy Consolo. After sides were chosen, we would go at it until it was almost dark. We played every game as if it was the last game of the World Series. Small verbal skirmishes would break out over closely disputed rulings on the field.

"What? Are you blind? He was safe by a mile!"

"No way! I had the ball waiting for him when he got here."

This type of petty haggling went on the whole game, and if we couldn't resolve the issue we would take turns getting our way on close calls. We didn't have any umpires, so most disputed plays were negotiated between the captains of each team. Fair play was an important part of the game that kids learned through trial and error. You learned never to argue about a disputed play if you knew in your heart you were wrong. It was a life lesson on "the playground honor system," a mandatory class communicated and imparted by everyone who played sports at Rancho.

We instinctively learned respect and integrity for the game and sportsmanship. If we couldn't win fair and square, then it wasn't worth winning. Winning didn't take precedent over sticking to our core principle of adhering to the rules. After all, we had to return and face each other the next day. Overly organized sports and closely supervised play make those sorts of lessons much harder for boys to truly learn today.

We got to know each other and bonded at an early age. We learned the other players' strengths and weaknesses. When it was getting dark and one team was behind, they would plead, "Come on! Let's play one more inning, just one more inning!"

No one wanted to ride his bike home without a decisive victory because it meant being branded a loser. If someone did leave without winning, they yelled, "We'll get you guys tomorrow and kick your butts."

Pickup baseball was where you started if you wanted to play baseball at a basic level or just practice your skills to improve your game. Most of the boys who regularly played baseball against each other in pickup games at Rancho were average to good athletes. I was well coordinated as a young boy and fit in nicely with the other athletes my age. I had excellent hand-eye coordination but lacked the upper body strength of some of the other boys. Most of us who were the same age were all fairly equal in our competitive sports skills.

However, at the top of the food chain of all the athletes was the one and only Billy Consolo. There wasn't anything average about him. He was exceptionally skilled in every aspect of any game. His agility was as good as any athlete anywhere and any age.

Billy belonged to a family of three boys who were very good athletes in their own right. Horace Consolo was his older brother, and Bobby was younger than Billy. They were a close knit family, and all three brothers looked out for each other. If you had a beef with one, you would have to take on the whole clan. For obvious reasons, very few tried to mess with the Consolos.

At Rancho playground I first witnessed the magical appeal of Billy Consolo and, like every other kid there, I wanted to be his friend. His wide welcoming smile lured me into his fast moving world, and I felt both comfortable and excited to be part of it. Once he got to know you, he treated you like his best friend, even if you knew you weren't.

I also connected with Billy at my school, of all places. Being a Catholic, his parents sent him to my school on Saturdays and after school for religious instruction so he could partake in his First Holy Communion. I was in the same class, which lingered for about three months, pummeling us with boring religious dogma and an unending litany of stories about biblical history.

We who attended Catholic school were obligated to wear uniforms as the nuns frowned on individuality. Those coming from the public schools were inclined to wear more casual attire. Billy was one of the boys who dared to wear Levis to school and for religious instruction.

The metal rivets on the back pockets of Levi jeans played havoc with the school desks, scarring the seats with deep grooves. Of course, this drove the nuns crazy since scratching their precious shiny desk seats was like destroying valuable antiques. So the boys who wore jeans—girls didn't wear jeans to school in those days—to the religious instruction classes were not allowed to sit at a desk.

"You should not wear jeans to religion class, William," a nun informed him one day.

"Why?" he asked calmly.

"They do not show proper respect."

"But I only have one other pair, my Sunday pants," he explained.

The nun replied, "Well, if you wear jeans, you sit on the floor."

So, they made him sit on the floor for the three months of religious instruction. Billy took it in stride with his usual smile and never complained about it. I think he was happy not to be going to Catholic School. He couldn't take the pettiness of the nuns and how unaccommodating they were to the students. It was operated like a penny-pinching business without regard for the employees.

He mentioned it to me after the last class was over, "Those sumbiches made me sit on the floor the whole time. But they didn't break me!"

The naughty nuns had scored another triumph in their quest to place things above children!

Billy had a star quality and connected with everyone on a highly personal level. No one was exempt from feeling special while in his presence. His glib tongue and unique magnetism was an irresistible combination. You might say that he had the ability to light up a room, but in reality he had the uncanny ability to light up other people. Everyone simply felt good being around him, and everyone was better, on the field or off, when he was around. This young Italian boy from Cleveland had won me over for life!

Every day he played at Rancho, he was the first one selected, and most of the time he was captain of the team. Being the best athlete on the playground had its perks. At eleven years old he could hold his own playing against fifteen-year-old boys. Billy was also a champion chatterbox, which made him even more interesting as a person. He had something to say about everything and everybody.

Yet, he wasn't a know-it-all or an egotist. He was just loquacious; he loved to yak. Also, he loved to tease some of the more serious players by tweaking a cheek or pinching a butt. Teasing and kibitzing were his strong suit, and he was as deft at it as he was at playing all sports.

As we all grew older together, Billy became more proficient at identifying where his highly diversified gifts would take him. We all knew that his unquestionable physical forte would take him to the major leagues, but no one acknowledged that his sharp mental acuity surpassed his obvious physical prowess.

He was always in the middle of any laughter that was going on at the playground. The other players gravitated to him because wherever Billy Consolo was hanging out, so was the entertainment and merriment.

His favorite joke would always start out, "This drunk/blond/fat guy [the adjective changed according to who would be the butt of his joke] walks into a bar." Sometimes he would insert himself into the joke and become the punch line. He had the terrific ability to laugh at himself and nothing was off limits when it came to creating laughter. His entertaining, loving sprit permeated the playground and made it a special place for all of us to be.

Few people ever watched our games as spectators. Joe Maguire's father, a short Irishman who wore an overcoat and hat in the summer, was the only one who occasionally observed our games. Mr. Maguire would stand bundled up, silently scrutinizing everything his son Joe did on the field and taking mental notes. During dinner that night, Joe would be chastised for any mistakes he made that day. For the escape and the good food, Joe loved to eat at my house.

There were a lot of exceptional kids in addition to Billy that I remember from those days. Billie "Buckwheat" Thomas of *Our Gang* movie fame was one of the kids who frequented Rancho in the 1940s, and he filled the bill nicely as our resident Hollywood celebrity. He worked on the movie lots most of the time, so he wasn't able to come every day. He would be driven up to the playground by a professional chauffer, which, of course, impressed the heck out of us. We'd stand there gawking like we were waiting for Humphrey Bogart or Rita Hayworth to step out onto the red carpet. Instead, a skinny black kid would step out to greet his adoring public. He was always welcomed with open arms and loving hugs. And, even better, he always had shiny new equipment available for us to use on the field.

Another class A talent was Eddie Palmquist, who had a major league arm at twelve years old and later pitched for the Los

Angeles Dodgers. Eddie at that age was already over six feet tall and weighed about 160 pounds—in contrast to the rest of us who averaged about 125 pounds. He was the biggest kid on the playground and possessed a golden right pitching arm, even though he was also known for his zany clowning around and off the wall personality. He threw a "heavy" ball that stung your hand when you played catch with him. He and Billy Consolo had natural physical abilities well beyond the rest of us. We held these two guys up as our example of what we wanted to become in our baseball lives.

We loved Eddie, especially if he was picked for our team, but hated to hit against him if he played for the other side. His fast ball was much too advanced for our age group, although he was around our same age. Lucky for us, he didn't pitch every day because when he did, he would blow us away with his fast ball. He also could saw off your bat, leaving you holding half a piece of wood if you didn't hit the ball on the sweet spot.

George Anderson joined the playground group in 1945. He was a scrappy, fun-loving athlete who had the proverbial "fire in the belly" attitude. He was a high-energy kid who carried a temper with a short fuse. A highly excitable individual, Georgie, as he was known in those days, was a fearless warrior who would battle you on the baseball field or roll you around on the grass in a wrestling match. Whatever he undertook, he did it with flair; he put 100 percent of his considerable intensity into playing baseball and having fun.

When George gained the nickname of Sparky later on as a professional, no one knew his real first name. In a crowded ballpark full of fans yelling "Sparky," if he heard someone holler "George," he would turn around and seek that person out because he knew that it was a friend from the old days. He was rarely called Sparky by his friends from the playground. In fact, the nickname Sparky never fit the incredibly classy person who George Anderson really was to us. You don't give a highly revered statesman a name usually reserved for a sports mascot. As he said, laughing at himself, "The only other one I've ever known named Sparky was a dog."

The name was hung on him by some sports broadcaster or writer for a rowdy incident that occurred during the heat of a game. What you do during a wild confrontation in a game is not who you are as a human being. It's troublesome when someone like a sportswriter gives a player a nickname that he doesn't even know and it sticks with him for life. There are still people in this world who don't know that George Anderson and Sparky Anderson is the same person. George will never be "Sparky" to me! He is referenced as Sparky in this book only because it is his identity to the public.

For his size, George was as tough as they came when engaging in fisticuffs. He didn't look for a fight, but you didn't want to start one with him. He was known as the antidote for bullies on the playground because he would not hesitate to take one down if one of them picked on a friend. The bullies steered clear of him as they knew better than to mess with the feisty one.

He had the type of devil-may-care nature that you didn't want to challenge, either on the baseball field or in a fight. His badge of courage was a black eye that he sported regularly on either eye. He feared no one and would never give up. You would have to knock him out or kill him. Usually his opponent just became exhausted, gave up, and usually regretted having fought him. The word was out on the playground; if you wanted to pick a fight with someone, don't pick it with Georgie Anderson.

Even with all these rough edges, he had a loving, infectious personality that was compelling to all that knew him. He could charm and befriend you with his contagious laughter and ready smile ... or he could knock you on your ass. Your call!

George was around ten or eleven years of age when he first came across Billy Consolo on the playground and their loving bond was immediately cast in stone.

Billy would say of George, "That little sumbich is a tough cookie!"

They became inseparable buddies for Billy's lifetime, and their love for each other was powerful. Their friendship would later take them to the Major Leagues together.

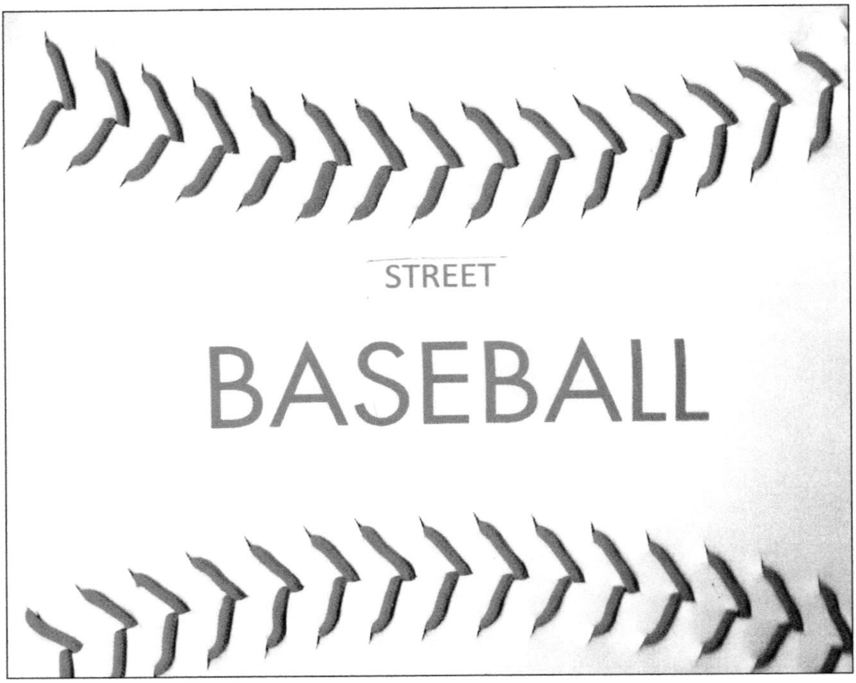
STREET
BASEBALL

6

Doing the Right Thing

WHEN WE NEIGHBORHOOD KIDS WEREN'T playing "serious" baseball on the playground, we were usually playing sandlot ball on the vacant lots of our neighborhood. At the end of my block there was an odd shaped triangular lot that was our particular favorite. It was not a buildable piece of land, but its shape was perfectly reminiscent of a baseball diamond with the streets on all sides to serve as the outfield. It was a nifty miniature baseball field. We got permission to build a backstop at the rear of the lot and to put bases around the infield. We would get together and play a quick pickup game when it wasn't convenient to trek off to the playground.

If you hit the ball straight toward center field, there was plenty of room, but if you pulled the ball to either left or right field, it was rather tight with houses swallowing up any ball hit in their direction. Up until this fateful day, we had been lucky; we had never broken a window.

There were about six of us playing "work-up" that day. All of us took turns at various positions, working our way up to bat. If a kid made an out, he retreated to the outfield to work his way back up to bat again. After toiling in the outfield for a while, I finally worked my way up to bat and was eager to get a solid hit.

My goal was to hit the ball toward centerfield where there were wide open spaces for the ball to travel untouched by defensive players. I swung and hit the ball squarely on the sweet spot of my bat. However, I swung a little late, and the ball did not go in the direction I had intended. A long fly ball headed for far left field, where houses happened to be permanently positioned! As the ball left my bat, I exclaimed, "Oh, no! The ball is headed for that house!" Immediately, I wanted to shout for a do–over but knew it was too late.

Of all the houses in the neighborhood you didn't want to hit, that house was the most dreaded one. I cringed and contorted my body, hoping that I could change the ball's trajectory simply by wishing it so. Nevertheless, like a heat-seeking missile, the ball locked directly onto its target. Not only did the ball hit that house, it managed to locate the huge, stained glass bay window displayed proudly on the front of the house. The ball shattered a very ornate, expensive section of the windowpane. It would have cost about five hundred dollars to replace it at a time when the average income was less than five hundred dollars per month.

Far more worrisome than the financial ramifications, though, was who lived inside the house. The house was owned by Jack Dragna, the purported head boss of the West Coast Mafia! Many frightening thoughts ran through my mind. What would be my fate? Would his mafia henchmen set my feet in cement and throw me into the Pacific? Would they point a machine gun out of a car and mow me down as I rode my bike to school? I imagined the Boss' angry tirades as I was dragged in to face the Italian tribunal, a court judged by Mafiosi. I envisioned them yelling and pointing at me, declaring me guilty before the trial even started.

My first instinct was to run like hell, and many of my friends did just that. I was left standing with the other Italian, Billy Consolo. He looked at me with eyes that said, "Boy, do I feel sorry for you!" I stood there frozen and unable to move, internally debating whether to sprint the two hundred yards to my home or to walk across the street to meet my fate. With his eyes as round as flying saucers, Billy asked, "What are you going to do? Run or face the mob?"

In my memory, the theme from the movie *The Godfather* played in the background. I was a blink away from tears, but I sucked up some courage with Billy by my side.

"What do you think? I can't run! As easy as it would be to run, it would only make me feel worse. I'll get a job caddying at the golf course and pay it off!"

Billy nodded his head. "I think you're doing the right thing. You can't outrun the mob!" But Billy wasn't about to hang around to see the scenario play out. "I'm splitting, man! I don't want to be here for the fireworks and bloodshed!"

Billy's comments didn't make me feel any better. I was suffering as much as anyone could with an overwhelming sense of guilt and dread. As Billy turned to head for his bike, he looked backward with a serious expression, adding, "Oh, and see if you can get my ball back!"

Getting his ball back was the least of my worries. I had to deal with the "Boss of Bosses" of the West Coast Mafia. As I walked toward the house, my knees felt like cooked spaghetti. I was expecting the worst possible confrontation. I thought of a few lame excuses to defend myself but decided to plead guilty because I knew I was dead meat.

I walked up to the front door, took a deep breath and rang the doorbell. It seemed like a lifetime before the front door opened. Standing in front of me was a handsome young man wearing a broad smile on his face and holding a baseball in his right hand. I started to speak, but gibberish came out instead of words, "Ah, I, ea, we were … aaah!" Before I could get a comprehensible word out of my mouth, he interrupted, "Boy, you really hit that ball a long way. You must be one of the stars in the neighborhood."

I got some courage from his words and offered, "I'm very sorry about the window. I want to pay for it because it was all my fault. Please forgive me for breaking your window."

I was short of verbal skills at that point and threw myself on the mercy of the one-man court. This judge turned out to be more compassionate than I would have ever imagined.

"Oh, you're forgiven. No problem. And don't worry about the window. We'll take care of it. I never liked the way it looked anyway."

He extended his right hand, gripping the baseball that he had found on his front room floor. I glanced at the errant baseball and noticed a minute sliver of glass sticking out of the stitching. Billy was getting his ball back, alright, but not without some remnants of the "big bang," as it has come to be known.

"Here," he said as he handed me the ball. "I have no use for this window crasher, and it looks to have quite a few more hits left in it. But do me one favor; keep swinging for the fences and have fun doing it."

I was struck dumb with no words to express my gratitude. I was overwhelmed with relief that came from an unexpected source. At that point, the Mafia and I were *famiglia,* and I felt extremely warm and proud to be of Sicilian heritage.

I found out later that the man I had dealt with was not Jack Dragna, but his son Frank, who was not in the "family business." At the time, Frank Dragna was a student at USC, attending on the GI Bill. USC would later be my alma mater. Frank had returned from the War as a decorated hero, having received the Purple Heart, among other impressive metals for bravery. Frank didn't need to show me any medals to prove himself to me. His actions that day demonstrated the class and kindness of a man who would forever be my hero.

I always wondered if it would have been different if Jack Dragna had answered the front door instead of his son. I'll never know, but, needless to say, I certainly appreciated the way it turned out.

I full heartedly thanked Frank Dragna, and if we hadn't been complete strangers, I would have given him big fat kisses on each cheek. Upon leaving the house I sprinted home with Billy's baseball in my glove, my feet never touching the ground. I ran into my house where my mother was ironing. I greeted her with a big smile, and she asked, "What are you so happy about?" Then she answered her own question. "I know! You must have hit a home run today!" My mother could always read my emotions, thus intuiting the contents of my sports-filled day. She knew there had been a special occurrence during that day. I just smiled and said, "Yeah. That's about right."

I now am sure that I was smiling so brightly that day, not because I had gotten away with something, but because I had learned such a valuable lesson about the value of decency. Of course, Frank Dragna had shown his kindness and mercy to me, which was a happy surprise. But far more importantly, I had done the right thing. I had overcome a deep seated urge to run away, and I had instead faced the consequences squarely in the face. Getting pardoned was icing on the cake, but the real reward was knowing that I was a good kid who was willing to take responsibility. That was better than a homerun in Yankee stadium any day.

I fully credit baseball for giving me the courage and conviction to do the right thing that day. One could argue that I might have done the right thing with or without baseball, but I think baseball, when played with its true spirit intact, teaches the value of fairness in a way that few other games do. A guy doesn't run from a broken window because the unspoken honor system of baseball says that he shouldn't. Life, baseball taught us, should be fair and honorable. However you hit the ball, you simply accepted its trajectory and its effects on your batting averages.

And for a lot of us, those hours on the field were like a refuge from the lessons of the streets, lessons that would instead have taught us to look out only for number one and to grab as much as we could. George Anderson, later to become the famous professional baseball manager nicknamed "Sparky," once recalled that in fifth grade a group of his buddies decided to break into a gas station. George refused because he had a baseball game already scheduled that day. The rest of the kids ended up serving a stint in juvenile hall for the gas station caper. George went on to become one of the winningest Major League Baseball managers of all time and was widely known for his down-to-earth dedication to honor and fairness in the game. One can only hypothesize how this kid's life would have differed without baseball.

To one level or another, this was true for all of who played together in those days. We all learned so much about life together, and, thus, these were our true brothers. No nun or schoolmaster could have taught us through books and lessons what we learned intuitively simply by playing a game that we loved. It was like these lessons became integrated into the fibers of our muscles.

• • • • • • • • • •

THE TEN RATHER ELDERLY MEN sitting on top of Secret Mesa in Sedona were ready to offer their last respects to Billy Consolo. There I was once again among my brothers—these boys with whom I had learned all the really important lessons of life. These lessons were timeless and infinite in significance, so it seemed impossible that we were now at the other end of life. Somehow, you think these people will always be there, yet here we were saying good-bye to Billy Consolo, the most undefeatable human being we had ever known.

But now he was gone. We knew if he could go, all of us could. By this time, death was not unique to our baseball squad; the ranks had been dwindling for the last three years. Besides Billy, Bobby Morris and Joe Maguire had passed on to join Gordy Sherett and

"Red" Zander, both of whom had left us many years ago at young ages. Another teammate, Warren Appley, had disappeared from the face of the earth and no one knew if he was dead or alive. Later, one of our teammates, Don Kenway, received confirmation that he was indeed gone. So with our team six men short, there were ten of us left to trek to the top of the hill, carrying with us the memories of our lifelong buddy.

In spite of the somber nature of our task, the mood was somewhat light and easy. Some of the guys were a little unsure of what was going to transpire during the hilltop gathering. I'm sure the prospect of Sedona New Age hooey made some of them a little nervous. Since I was the one who had organized this unusual way of saying good-bye to Billy, I tried to start the ball rolling by standing in the center of the circle without putting pressure on any one person.

"Who would like to speak first about knowing and loving Billy Consolo or share anything that you learned from being a teammate or friend of his?" I asked.

There was a silent pause for about thirty seconds since no one wanted to be the first to speak his thoughts about Billy. Then a familiar, raspy voice broke the silence. It came from the person that I suspected would be the first to talk about Billy. George "Sparky" Anderson was sitting with a dour expression on his face and his head hung low. Of all the guys on the team who had grown up with Billy, George was the closest to him. George had managed in the big leagues for twenty-six years, and for seventeen of them Billy had coached by his side in the dugout in Detroit.

When he left the Cincinnati Reds after winning two World Series and four pennants in the National League, George made the decision to take Billy with him to manage the Detroit Tigers (1979) in the American League. He said he needed someone he could trust and someone who could keep him grounded in the big leagues. He and Billy had known each other through Midget Baseball, high school ball, and the summer of American Legion baseball. He knew Billy better than his own brother, and they were definitely closer than brothers.

George "Sparky" Anderson

Together in Detroit they won one World Series (1984) and one American League title. With 2,194 wins under his belt, George ended up in Cooperstown, the Baseball Hall of Fame. After earning his big league salary and his championship rings, Billy would go on to prove further his athletic diversity, teaching golf in the west San Fernando Valley of Los Angeles. Yes, he also was a great, low-handicap golfer, as he taught and played the game until the day of his premature demise on March 27, 2008.

George's gravelly, deep voice cut through the desert air like a foghorn. "I met this little Italian boy when I first moved from South Dakota to Los Angeles in 1944. We were both ten years old, and you couldn't keep us off the baseball diamond. From the beginning, Billy was the best athlete I had ever seen and would ever see until I got to the big leagues. He was the finest high school baseball player I had ever seen and that is true to this day."

His voice started to crack with emotion as he started to sob uncontrollable tears. George is the only man I've ever known who could cry and speak at the same time and still be understood by everyone. At Billy's funeral service seven months earlier, he had delivered a heart-wrenching eulogy, crying throughout the whole presentation. There wasn't a dry eye in the church, including the priest. He spoke choked up and sobbing, but every word came out loud and clear.

"He was everything to me: my brother, my son, my best friend, my confidant, my sounding board. We were as close as two people could get and not be Chinese twins. He was with me in this life for fifty-six years, and when I join him, it will be forever. Next to my wife Carol, he is the person I have trusted and loved the most. I will miss him as long as I can breathe. When I was managing with him in Detroit for seventeen years, I never had to worry where he was; he was always beside me, supporting me, and I know he's beside me now." He lifted his gray-white head and tears were streaming down his wrinkled cheeks.

This man, George Anderson, had done it all. He'd been to the summit of baseball success and back and had lost his copilot in life. No one felt worse about Billy's passing than him, and he had set the emotional bar high for the rest of us. The raspy-voiced one, who at this moment possessed an uncharacteristically high level of eloquence and grammatical skill, finished his soliloquy without a single double negative or dangling participle.

Another renowned athlete from the City of the Angels, Frank Layana, was the next to speak. Frank was a two-sport, all-American high school super athlete from Loyola High School on Venice Boulevard in the heart of Los Angeles. He was a first-team high school all-American fullback. He was also a star baseball player, excelling both in the outfield and on the pitching mound. Although there were no radar guns in those days to read the velocity of a fastball, it was estimated that Frank threw at around ninety miles per hour. He won football scholarships from every major college in the country, most notably USC and Notre Dame. However, he opted to sign a professional baseball contract right out of high school for sixty thousand dollars, which was a hell of a lot of money in those days when the average personal income was about five hundred dollars per month.

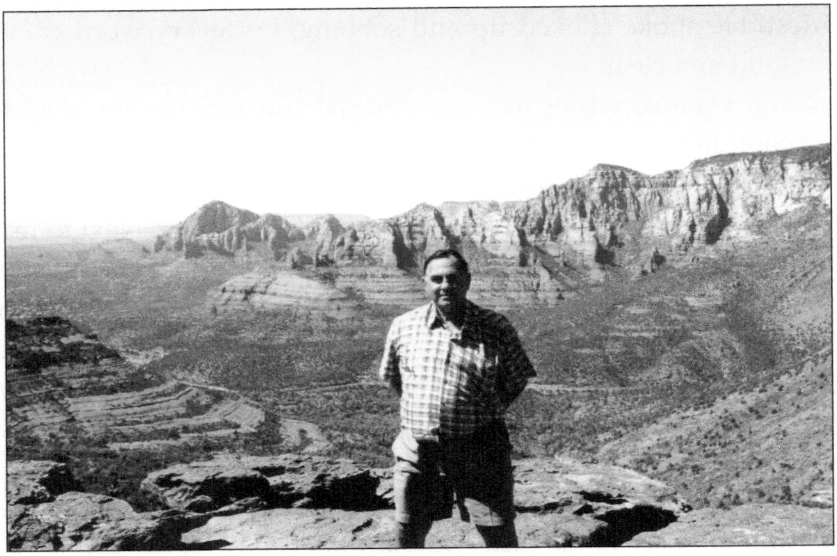

Frank Layana

He immediately married his high school sweetheart, Carole Malloy, and the couple started having babies one after another. After Frank's baseball career was over, his job as a construction supervisor took him all over the world, so he was away from home a lot. Twenty-five years after Frank separated from Carole, he became openly religious. When he retired, he moved to Thailand for financial and health reasons.

When we first gathered on the rocks, Frank sat down on the hard sandstone and looked to be very uncomfortable because of his size. In high school he was six foot two, and about 180 pounds of solid muscle. Now at seventy-three years of age, he had ballooned to around three hundred pounds and had trouble walking because of his bad knees. He wanted to get both knee joints replaced, but doctors refused because of his overweight condition.

He spoke in a deep voice with emotion dripping from every word.

"I loved Billy. He was my soul brother. When I heard about his passing, I was devastated. I called George Anderson from Thailand, and we both cried over the phone for an hour. I thought I would not have to endure this sad day because I thought for sure I would go before Billy."

He looked out over the photogenic panorama of red rocks before him, transfixed for a moment by the splendor of Cathedral Rock and the cumulous clouds forming around it, and then returned his gaze downward. His emotions were bubbling over with the loss of an athlete equal to, if not better, than himself. He had lost someone even he could look up to in awe.

With soulful eyes he continued, "Billy was a one-of–a–kind athlete and human being. He was such a giving person, and he was so entertaining that I could listen to his stories all day ... and I did. It's hard to think of our great Legion team without Billy. He was the heart and soul of our team, our best clutch hitter. He had star quality in everything he did and lived life with love and respect for everyone he met. I will pray for him every day of my life. Good-bye, my friend."

Frank wiped the stream of tears from his eye sockets before they could drop to the sandstone.

HERE ARE THE LADS who lived up to their name and literally struck "terror" in the hearts of their opponents during the recent junior baseball play at Rancho Cienega playground. This is the Terrors baseball team, sponsored by the Southwest Optimist club. Members (bottom row, left to right) Landy, Beggs, Morris, Thombs, (second row) Ex, Corbolo, Feser, L. Whitehead, (top row) Shaine Wilson, Fish, T. Whitehead, and Crowley. Absent were Ed Palmquist and Carl Magie. The Terrors tomorrow meet the American League champions, the Hardshells in a "little world series" play-off.

—Jon Charles Photo.

1946 Los Angeles City Midget League champions

7

The Terrors of Los Angeles

IN THE FIRST MONTH OF 1947, a gruesome event that captured national print and radio headlines shook our quiet, peaceful neighborhood. On January 15, a dead body was discovered on a vacant lot on Norton Avenue, three blocks west of my home on Olmsted Avenue. Mutilated and severed at the waist, the remains of Elizabeth Short, who would be nicknamed the Black Dahlia, was happened upon by neighbors who were on a daily stroll.

The incident deeply alarmed our Leimert Park community. The collective state of fear grew to the point where no one would leave their homes at night. And during the day people refused to go near Norton Avenue, either by foot or by car. The kids in the neighborhood, including me, would not dare to ride their bikes within blocks of the macabre crime scene. The details we had heard and the stories we read in the papers were enough to give any kid nightmares for months. My younger sister, Phyllis Jean, was so affected by the hideous event that she wouldn't even go to the bathroom without an escort.

The mutilation-murder instantly changed Leimert Park residents into a frightened and introverted group of people. For the first time, everyone locked their doors day and night. No one walked alone anymore, and for a while people didn't drive alone. A shadow had been cast over our little pocket of a paradise. The lady who was murdered had recently relocated from Hyde Park in Boston, Massachusetts. For a while, she was just another statistic amongst the hordes of people swarming into Southern California from the East Coast and Midwest who wanted to make it in Hollywood. Now she had found her fame, but hardly in the way she had wanted.

The unsolved Black Dahlia murder generated persistent speculation across the country and eventually gave rise to several best-selling books and film depictions. Strangely, approximately sixty people have since confessed to the sixty-three-year-old unsolved crime. The confessors were mostly men, but several women came forward as well.

Years passed before Leimert Park recovered from that terrifying nightmare, and the people returned to living normal lives. Luckily, frequenting the Rancho playground didn't necessitate riding our bikes past Norton Avenue. We took a straight journey west on Santa Barbara Avenue to the park and tried not to think about the atrocities around the corner. We were more than happy to escape to our athlete's Elysian fields.

Our playground director, Benny Lefebvre, established an innovative summer league that year at our playground. The teams that he formed competed for the right to play against the best players from other playgrounds in the area. The ultimate goal for any team was to be named Los Angeles City Champion.

Although Benny formed the teams, we played without coaches, without parental interference, without knowledge of baseball strategy, without decent equipment, and without umpires. No one had any idea how to organize a team, but everyone managed to pull themselves together and show up every Saturday morning to play a game in one of the four corners of the enormous field.

There was no organizational structure to muck up the fun we had prepared for ourselves.

I don't remember how the teams were chosen, but, however it happened, it resulted in a big blunder. One of the teams had Eddie Palmquist and Billy Consolo together on the same roster. It was definitely a political faux pas because they were probably the two best baseball players in the whole city, let alone our playground. What in the world were they doing on the same team?

At any rate, I was ecstatic when I found out that I had been placed on the same roster with them. No matter who else was playing with us, with those two players on our side we couldn't lose. Yet, even with those two stars playing with me, I decided that I was going to contribute to our group and make it even better. I wasn't about to show up and allow the stars to win games without my help. It would have been too easy just to turn up every game and be a bit player, but that's not what I had in mind. I wanted to excel with them!

Further contributing to the imbalance, we had some other good ballplayers placed on our team. Our players consisted of fifteen members, all of whom were regular playground attendees. We had played baseball together for years at Rancho and in the streets, so we knew what everyone was capable of doing on the baseball field. We named our team the Terrors because we knew we would strike terror in the hearts of our opponents. There were about 350 boys playing baseball on our playground alone.

Every Saturday morning, we met at Benny's office to pick up our one game ball and catcher's equipment. Then the two teams would walk to one of the four baseball diamonds to play the game. Throughout the day, games were played simultaneously on all four diamonds. With no coaches, the games were played without any strategy—just hitting, fielding, and throwing. Bunting was non-existent; no one wanted to waste an at bat by bunting a ball. We would commandeer a high school student as an umpire, and he called all the close plays at the bases as well as the balls and strikes.

It was about as unorganized and as wild as baseball could possibly get, but we were having the time of our lives. There were no parents in the bleachers watching the game. In fact, there was no one watching at all, except for Mr. Maguire. He would stand behind the batting cage wearing his overcoat, galoshes, and hat, watching his son Joe play. We were accustomed to playing without anyone in the stands, so it didn't bother us. We would laughingly say, "We're playing before ten thousand nail heads today, so play hard!"

Our team was so good, it was almost a joke. No one even came close to us. We had great hitting, we had the best pitching, and we had speed to burn. We had it all. Of course, our ultimate weapons were Consolo and Palmquist, two of the best athletes in the city. But baseball for us wasn't all about winning; it was mainly about bonding as a team, improving our skills, and having some fun. But, then again, as Billy Consolo would repeatedly say, "It's a lot more fun to win than to lose."

No one knew more about winning than "Billy C.," who played on championship teams all through school until he reached the big leagues. He, Eddie Palmquist, and George "Sparky" Anderson played high school baseball together at Dorsey High School and won the Los Angeles City Championship in 1950. Having played together for two years, to this day they hold the city's high school record for their forty-two consecutive wins over a two-year period.

We Terrors did in fact terrify the competition, storming through our league unbeaten in the first ten games. And then it happened; Eddie Palmquist left on summer vacation one week with his parents. Without his blazing fastball on the mound, we Terrors endured our first loss of the summer. We were all very upset and the talkative Billy Consolo protested, "Well, I'll be a sumbitch! What's wrong with him? Doesn't he know summer is the worst time to take a vacation? It's when baseball is played!" Of course, no one told his parents that important bit of information because they always took their vacation in summer like everyone else!

When Eddie returned the next week, we picked up where we left off before his departure and resumed our winning ways. Billy wouldn't let anyone take any more vacations. We finished our regular season play with a thirteen and one record, which was by far the best on the playground. Now it was time for the Terrors to compete against the American League winner.

George "Sparky" Anderson had played in the American League for the Cardinals but his team lost their last game and came in second in their league. The Cardinals were done for the season. George came out to watch our games since all of his best buddies were on the Terror's team. Billy, Eddie, and George were a powerful triad, known to some as "the three amigos."

The winning team in the American League, the Hard Shells, ended the season with an eleven and three record. They had a super athlete on their team whose name was Frank Layana. He would later become a high school classmate of mine as well as our teammate on the American Legion team four years later.

The two teams were well matched, both being blessed with superior athletes who were well above the average players. We had a slight edge with Eddie Palmquist pitching and Billy Consolo playing third base for our Terrors. However, we got a scare in the very first inning as Frank Layana ripped a double into right center off Eddie Palmquist, driving in the first run of the game. I got a hit in our half of the first inning and then I stole second base, but I was left standing on second base as the inning ended.

We battled the Hard Shells without success until the fifth inning when Billy Consolo, Tom Fish, and I all got base hits to break open the game. Tom Fish was our catcher as he was the only one who could handle Eddie Palmquist's great fast ball. Tom had settled Eddie down after the first inning, and we took the lead 4–1 after five innings.

It still could have been a close game, but Eddie Palmquist wouldn't permit it. He shut down the Hard Shells the rest of the game, and we went on to win the city championship game 8–1. Billy Consolo, Tom Fish, Leonard Landy, and I led the attack with two hits apiece. It was to be Billy's and my first taste of a championship, and we liked the flavor!

Junior Baseball League Champs Play Tomorrow

With the last score in the final interleague game called, the Terrors, sponsored by the Southwest Optimist club, the Hardshells, flying the colors of Westside Paint Company and the Blackhawks have been declared official winners in the National, American, and midget leagues respectively, in junior baseball at Rancho Cienega. Play was completed last week.

The Terrors, boasting an almost perfect record of 13 wins and one loss, and the Hardshells, with an 11 and 3 standing will meet in one game this week to determine the ultimate champion.

Series, which opens tomorrow at 5 p.m. at Rancho, has been dubbed the "Little World Series." Later games are slated for Wednesday and Friday, same time, same place.

Presentation of trophies to the winning ball players will take place Friday noon at the Eleds restaurant, following a luncheon. Leagues have been sponsored by civic organizations and business houses in the community and are under the general supervision of the Crenshaw Civic Council.

National League

	W	L
Terrors (Optimists)	13	1
Lions (Lions)	11	3
Hawks (Lions)	8	6
Yankees (Crenshaw C of C)	8	6
Warriors (Kiwanis)	3	9
Dodgers (20-30)	3	11
Indians (Rotary)	0	14

Terrors Move Toward Gilmore

Rancho Cienega Terrors of the minor baseball league drove one step closer to the city championship Thursday by defeating the Manchester Cardinals 1 to 0. Ed Palmquist started for the Terrors and held his opponents to one hit while his pitching rival was knocked for one hit and six bases on balls.

The Terrors capitalized in the fifth inning on three walks and one hit to account for the lone tally of the game. The Terrors have one more game to play. If they win, they will go to Gilmore field for the city championship in September.

8

A Legion of Teams

SIXTEEN OF US WERE TO be selected to play on an American Legion baseball team. This was not just any baseball team. Every boy seventeen years old or younger wanted to be a member of this team. Since most of us had played together for many years, we knew each other's abilities, weaknesses, and strengths. We also knew that this was going to be a fun team. It was an opportunity to play on the same team with guys we had known all of our young lives. Anyone who played baseball and lived in the area wanted to be chosen to play with this group, but only sixteen players were allowed on each team, as mandated by American Legion Baseball.

Our playground director and designated coach of the team, Benny Lefebvre, had been working at Rancho La Cienega for years and had all the credentials to coach this team. He knew all the boys from years of watching us play on his field, and now he had the difficult task of selecting only sixteen players out of the sea of talent that flooded the park. Benny oversaw this breeding ground, one that spawned many great athletes from the area. He not only had the ability to develop athletic skill, but he could also spot young players who possessed latent talent.

He organized sports leagues for baseball and football and

worked to develop talented young players. He was the perfect choice to coach our team as he had been tutoring playground youngsters for years. Benny was not only a very good coach; he also was blessed with excellent organizational skills.

We all anxiously awaited Benny's two-day tryout camp where sixteen exceptional players would be chosen. He probably knew who he was going to select as his first ten choices, so the two day tryout camp would help him sort the wheat from the chaff. He needed to find six players to round out the team. I knew I stood a chance, but no one could say who would make it. I was a jumble of excitement and anxiety.

During the tryout period, Benny put us through a succession of grueling workouts to see who could hold up under pressure. He loved speed, and he would clock us with a stopwatch as we circled the bases. He would have us run competitive sprint races until our tongues hung out. If you were slow, you didn't have much chance to make Benny's team, unless you were a catcher. The catcher was usually the stockiest guy on the team who weighed the most and, therefore, was the slowest.

To discover who had good arm strength, he would have us throw long distances to the bases from all over the field. If you were accurate with a strong arm, that was a plus. Outstanding defensive skills would place you high on Benny's selection list. He would hit fly balls over our heads and yell, "Go get it! Go get it! That ball should have been caught!"

We would chase balls down with great speed and agility, and then return the ball to Benny with a strong, accurate throw. He would yell at us, "You gotta play defense! Defense wins baseball games!"

We took batting practice until our hands had blisters and the bat felt like it had lead in it. Hitting was our forte. We loved watching the ball jump off our bats and fly to the deep part of the field. Billy Consolo was very strong and had a quick bat, and he could hit the ball the farthest. When he took batting practice, everyone stopped to watch him. We knew we were watching a special athlete do what he did best—hit a baseball.

Bunting practice was an event that Benny watched very closely because it was a skill most of us neglected to practice on our own. When we played on the streets and on the playground, no one bunted; everyone wanted to blast the ball as far and hard as possible. If we tried to bunt, we would be laughed out of the game. Now bunting would be an essential part of Benny's winning strategy, so he wanted to witness who was able to properly execute a bunt. Not many of the kids could, but those who could consistently lay down a bunt in practice would make the team.

The competition was fierce, and some unconditioned players couldn't take it, so they dropped out. One of the dropouts was heard saying, "What team are we trying out for? The Olympics?"

Benny smiled and shrugged his shoulders but made no comment, leaving us without any praise for our efforts. After the tryout, he would tell us as we were leaving, "If you can't make the effort in practice, you won't make it in a game."

Benny wanted to establish who was willing to put forth the extra effort it would take to achieve the goal he had in mind. Most of the players were not happy about the way things turned out when they learned they were not among the fortunate chosen few, the "sweet sixteen."

There were many young ballplayers who rode their bikes home the last day with broken hearts and tears in their eyes after sixteen anointed ones were selected out of around forty boys who had auditioned for a spot on the ball club.

I was elated to be picked as one of the sixteen boys chosen to represent our playground in the American Legion Baseball system with 16,299 other teams. To be picked to play on this team placed you in an elite category of the boys who showed up to play on the playground. I had expected to be picked, as I was an above average ballplayer, though not on a par with some of our more gifted players. I had always thought of myself as a strong support player, not the main guy you build a team around, like a Billy Consolo or a Frank Layana.

With my level of talent, I could do all the things that the great players could do, just not as well. My only self-doubt was that I might not be good enough to make the starting nine. I was on the team, but was I going to play much? Benny knew what quality of ballplayers we were because he had been watching us since we were in the Midget League. He already had his starting team picked, and I was one of them!

When Benny finally finished separating the culls from the cream of the crop, we had accumulated a diverse mix of nationalities and characters unlike any other group of seventeen-year–old boys. The team consisted of German, Irish, Italian, Jewish, English, Basque, Norwegian, and some of unknown origin, and, of course, we were coached by a Frenchman named Benny Lefebvre.

We lived in a cross section of the LA neighborhoods, a middle-class melting pot of every known religion and ethnicity. We developed a mutual respect for each other's abilities as ballplayers that transcended ethnic preconceptions. We didn't care what church you attended or what color you were; we only wanted to know how well you played the game of baseball.

Two notable guys we played with on the playground who didn't make the team were Billie "Buckwheat" Thomas, one of the little rascals from the *Our Gang* movies, and Howard "Howie" Weitzman, who would later gain fame as the main defense lawyer in the John DeLorean and Michael Jackson trials. Some very good ballplayers, including Tom Fish, weren't chosen to play on the team simply because they were a couple months too old. Tom was a close friend of mine, and I was disappointed not to have him as a teammate.

When the last selected team member was scribbled on Benny's roster list and everyone finished congratulating each other, Benny called us around him for an opening day get-to-know-each-other pep talk. But he was reminded by George Anderson, "We already know each other, so let's get on with the business of hitting and fielding."

Benny was fully aware that we knew each other, but he wanted to deliver a special message to grab our attention. On our first day practicing as a newly formed team, he wanted to begin preparing us for the long, tough expedition he had laid out for us. Benny started his sermon looking into each of our eyes with religious zeal. There were times he looked like a monk or priest as he talked.

"Each of you has been picked for a reason, and that reason is that we want a team, not a group of sixteen good, individual players. If I didn't think you were team players, I wouldn't have chosen you. And if we misjudged you, and you aren't a team player, you can leave now with no hard feelings."

No one dared flinch.

Benny continued, "I feel we have the right players in the right positions to go all the way."

That last statement caught everyone by surprise, and we began to squirm and look around in uncertainty. We struggled with the esoteric idea of "all the way" on our first day together. We were collectively thinking, "Why would Benny say that on our first day of practice, when we haven't even played our first ballgame yet?" Benny's statement was the first of many blunt but perplexing remarks he would throw our way.

"On this first day of practice, I want each of you to think of our goal as winning the National Championship." He looked intently around the group into each of our eyes. "Think..." he said, pausing to point his index finger to his temple, "all the way!"

• • • • • • • • • •

HE ALLOWED US A MOMENT to acclimate to that idea and then went on, "Henry Ford once said, 'Coming together is a beginning. Keeping together is progress. Working together is success.'"

"We're on the third step, 'working together for success.' You can't achieve your goals unless you work together. This summer you will learn to work as a team, and as a result baseball will become much more fun. However, it will be a hard chore to learn to play baseball in a new way. The new way includes taking responsibility for your job on the team. Everyone on the squad will have a job to do, and if everyone does their work properly, we will have a successful season. You will be working very hard, and you won't always understand some of the new things we will be trying."

He took a long pause and let us digest that mouthful of words.

"There is one last thing that I want you to think about and carry in your hearts through the summer. Every day we're together and you have a ball, bat, or glove in your hand, I want you to believe in your hearts that we can win the National Championship. It's like a prayer. You must repeat it daily, like brushing your teeth, and believe it in the core of your soul. Winning starts with believing you can do it. If you can't do that, then you should give up your spot on this team to another player."

No one even bothered listening to that last statement. Nobody was leaving this team! We all looked up at Benny and then at each other with confusion in our eyes. Was he putting us on, or was he determined to convince us that this team actually had a chance to win the American Legion national championship? There were 16,299 other teams around the country in the American Legion system. Did we hear him accurately? Did we have a chance to win it all?

I did some quick math, calculating the numbers needed to win it all. I came up with roughly forty games to be played during the summer to take us into September. To make it even more demanding, we couldn't lose more than five games during that summertime. Whoever won the national title in September had to complete a nearly impossible task.

Benny Lefebvre's brilliant coaching mind pulled a psychological coup as he released those optimistic words from his lips on the first official day of practice. He had "planted the seed of consciousness," although very small, in our young minds. And that seed would eventually sprout into the awareness that we had a group of talented, although raw, players that could compete with anyone in the country.

The new team talent included four All-League players, one City Player of the Year, and a host of exceptional support and backup players. However, for Benny to talk about winning the national championship on the first day of practice seemed outlandish to me. Especially when we were up against 16,299 other teams. Talk about a long shot!

Our American Legion sponsor was stitched on the new uniforms that we proudly wore—Los Angeles, Crenshaw Post 715. The uniforms were made of heavy grey flannel cotton fabric, which on hot days was torture to wear, but we weren't about to complain since some teams sported ratty, three-year-old uniforms. We figured it's better to be uncomfortable and look like pros than to be comfortable and look like bumpkins.

After all, baseball uniforms play an important role in the psychological ingredient of the game; first impressions are irreversible and have an immediate visual impact on your opponent. Whenever we played against a sloppily attired bunch of ballplayers, we knew we could jump all over them. Seeing your opponent as an ill-outfitted group gives you great confidence.

When we first tried on our new garb, we felt like major leaguers; putting on brand new baseball attire had that effect. After I first put on my uniform, I stood in front of the mirror for about a half hour and couldn't believe how good it looked on me. I turned around twice to make sure that there were no bulges where there shouldn't be and everything was picture perfect. I couldn't help staring into the mirror and complimenting my reflection. "Lookin' good, man! Lookin' good!" I was truly pleased with the way the new uniform fit my body. It didn't hurt that the girls at the playground would like it too!

Looking fine in your uniform was a prerequisite to being a decent ballplayer; you must look like a first-rate player to be one in your own mind. We felt that playing baseball without a suitable uniform was like attending church in a bikini bathing suit.

Most of us knew how to wear a baseball uniform, and those who did not were taught by those who did! It was an art. Looking sharp in our uniforms on the field as a group was the preemptive strike against your opponent for its intimidation factor. It showed the other side that your squad had a work ethic that started when you put on your uniform.

Playing baseball in the American Legion system during the summer months was a given since there was no other option. There were no other leagues to join. You either played in the American Legion league or you didn't play summer baseball. The American Legion's national program was very well organized and laden with sponsors eager to help young baseball players hone their skills for higher success.

The American Legion posts were filled with returning servicemen after World War II. Almost every post sponsored a baseball team, resulting in 16,300 ball clubs in the system. The reward at the end of the season for the one surviving team was a paid trip to the 1951 games three and four of the World Series in whichever city those games were played in October. At the time, that package was worth about $1,500 per player, depending upon where the World Series was being held that year. And if it were to be played in New York City, which looked probable the way the Yankees were playing, it would be more like $2,000 for each person. With sixteen players on a team, plus the business manager and a coach, it was a sizable amount of cash, and it was in the 1950s value of the US dollar.

And if that wasn't enough, the final four teams would compete for the national championship in Briggs Stadium, home of the Detroit Tigers professional baseball team. It all added up to a major carrot dangled in front of any team that hoped to outlast all other competitors. The American Legion was offering the world to a bunch of seventeen-year-olds who lived and breathed baseball and wanted nothing else but to play for our love of the game!

"You have to sacrifice your individual goals for the greater objective of the team."

"Give it up, give it up for the good of winning."

—Benny Lefebvre

9

Zen Ben

PRACTICES, UNDER THE WATCHFUL EYE of Benny Lefebvre, continued into early June of 1951. Day after day, he drilled us in the fundamentals of the game until we could execute essential basic plays in our sleep. But we would need more than fundamental baseball skills to win the national championship. To play at a higher level, we would have to discover talents we didn't know we had, and latent mental abilities would have to be mined from our disorganized juvenile minds. Benny Lefebvre would be the one to give us the cerebral enema we needed to succeed.

We had learned to play baseball on our own, relying on the raw instincts needed to compete on the streets and playgrounds. We had never been trained in the mental aspects of the game, and it showed in our mindless misdeeds on the field. Most of us didn't even know there was a mental side to playing baseball, but we were about to find out.

Yogi Berra, famous for his "creative" use of our English language, was credited with saying, "The game of baseball is 90 percent mental, and the other half is physical." We were playing 100 percent with the physical "half" of the game, and we didn't know anything about the other 90 percent.

Benny had his hands full as our mentor. He had to redirect our thought process away from personal stats. "You have to sacrifice your individual goals for the greater objective of the team." He would often remind us, "Give it up! Give it up for the good of winning." This hypothesis did not go over very well with our offensive-minded bunch.

"Why do we have to bunt? Let us just swing away; we can hit!" George yelled at the coach when he failed three attempts to lay down a bunt in practice. Benny lost his patience and shot back, "You won't get any batting practice until you learn how to bunt. Skillful bunting will win games. Base hits just fatten up your batting average."

Then he said something that flew right over our heads.

"When you overlook something that wins games, you're not looking at the right things." Huh? That sounded like gibberish to me.

At first, Benny's wisdom didn't resonate with us, but he never stopped teaching us. He kept preaching to us heathens. Eventually, after some moaning and complaining, we bought into a system of concepts that centered on unselfishness and teamwork. We had heard the word teamwork but had no idea how it worked on the ball field.

Benny believed the word teamwork was synonymous with the word winning. You couldn't have one without the other. His philosophy, slowly but surely, dug deep into our thought processes. He would reiterate almost daily, "Each team member is responsible for the entire team's growth as a functioning group. When one member of the group chooses to use his power of free will in ways that do not reflect the higher good of the team, then the whole team suffers." According to Benny, an unselfish player is like a well-oiled cog in a high-powered machine; a selfish player is like a wrench thrown into the works. If each of us contributed all our full mental awareness to mobilize the team to a high level of performance, a winning group could emerge.

An excellent example of team play is the turning of a double play, when the team makes two outs on one hit ball. It takes at least three infielders working in tandem, each touching and releasing the ball, to complete the play. If any player fails to do his job properly, it doesn't work. Benny would have us practice the double play until we became like gears in a Swiss watch. All thinking was extracted from it. It became as natural as breathing, so we could execute it even during the most stressful of situations.

Benny would be sure to point out that baseball lessons are life lessons. He'd say, "If you're not a team player, you won't last long in any functioning group. Golf is the only sport that doesn't require team play, but life is not a golf course. Just try telling your boss that you're not a team player and see what happens. You're gone!"

Then he would point to the exit gate on the field to indicate that we'd be on the outside of that gate looking in if we didn't heed his wisdom. In teaching us the principals of selfless winning, he made his expectations clear.

"Play together and you win. Play for yourself and you become a loser. It's not very popular to be a loner when your group is working toward a goal. Baseball is a sport where each player is relying on his teammates for their support, no one on this team will be valued above any other player. We're all one." These were the kinds of aphorisms Benny showered on our young brains, washing them clean of their selfish and prideful habits.

In today's world, you might call Benny a Zen master of sorts. Of course, nobody talked about that kind of stuff in those days and surely Benny had no knowledge of such philosophies. Rather, he had an instinctive, gut-level understanding of what it meant to stay in the moment and to get in the flow of the energy. Zen masters teach practitioners to completely dissolve into the activity at hand, which is exactly what Benny taught. We could have spent ten years in a Zen monk monastery without learning these concepts as well as he taught them. And to top it all off, he taught it to a bunch of seventeen-year-old kids.

Through Benny's not-so-subtle affirmations, we became aware of how much we didn't understand about the game of baseball. He trained our youthful, wandering minds to stay focused on baseball and only baseball. We didn't know it at the time, but we were embarking on a journey that would change the way we played and perceived the game of baseball.

""You no longer have to worry about your batting average because winning is the only thing that matters," he said with a straight face. The team was stunned by his anomalous statement; this was news to us.

I thought I had the perfect question that would challenge Benny's strange statement.

"Excuse me, Benny, but don't higher batting averages help a team win games?"

The meeting suddenly became seriously silent as everyone turned toward Benny for his answer to this important philosophical baseball question.

I stood there smugly, thinking myself quite the baseball genius. Apparently Benny was not as impressed with my question as I was with it.

"Scoring more runs than the other team wins games, which means focusing our strategy on scoring runs, not higher batting averages."

He took one more step toward being out-of-bounds of our comprehension.

"Guys, you must not mistake something you don't understand for reality."

One of the players thought he would score some brownie points with the coach and blurted out, "I think I'm starting to get the idea of this whole mental thing!" The rest of the team members looked at him like he had just totally lost brain function. Our minds were buried in overstimulation and confusion.

Having to release attachment to our beloved batting averages was the toughest concept we would have to swallow that summer.

In our minds, batting average was the most significant personal statistic in baseball. One of the main topics of conversation among the ballplayers was the question, "What are you hitting?" Hitting over or under the magic .300 mark defined who you were as a player. Each of us wanted to know where our own batting average fit into the pecking order of the team. Now Benny was telling us it didn't matter.

But Benny doggedly sold us on the idea of using a new strategy to score more runs. Runs were more important to our team, so for now figuring out our batting averages after each game was banned. As our minds let go of our batting averages, we all stopped thinking about "me" and started playing for "we."

Playing winning baseball at this level meant not only executing the fundamentals, but also playing with high awareness. By doing the little mental things that other teams overlooked, like backing up bases, throwing to the cutoff man instead of directly to home, and, of course, bunting.

If you wanted to play on this team, you learned to bunt, avoided mental errors that cost games, and gave up your own ego-driven inclinations. No one player was above the team, and we put aside our own personal ambitions for the benefit of the whole unit. Benny would say, "If you want to be valuable to this team, then play like it; play with intention."

And his intention was to win it all! And now that intention was ours too.

Benny was a stern Zen master who wouldn't tolerate any negativity toward his preaching, so we didn't resist what he was teaching us. It was mandatory to pull together as a cohesive unit. We were learning to think and strategize in ways that were necessary for us to win it all. As long as we were being offered this transformational journey, we might as well hop on the train and enjoy the ride. Anyway, if we wanted to play, it was Benny's way or no way!

• • • • • • • • • •

AS THE SEASON STARTED, BENNY had us whipped into shape, and we were ready to take on the world. He had us playing together with teamwork and high precision. He told us, "The way you're playing, there is only one team that can beat you and that is you. Force the other team to work hard to beat you. Don't give them any help!"

We must not have been listening because even with all of Benny's super coaching and our high-quality players, we still managed to lose the first game of the season to a team from Huntington Park, California, a suburb of Los Angeles. They were a good ball club, but we were better at every position, including pitching with our two impressive pitching stars. But sometimes, we learned, the best team doesn't deserve to win.

As prepared as we were that first day, our star pitcher, Frank Layana, couldn't find the plate with his fast ball. He wasn't following through with his pitches. This meant that he was not conscious of where the release point of the baseball was, due to the improper mechanics of his delivery motion. To make things worse, our catcher, Bill Lachemann, had three passed balls, which resulted in three unearned runs.

Frank's fastball was all over the batter's box, except in the strike zone, and "Lach," our catcher, couldn't handle the inconsistency of Frank's pitches, resulting in three balls getting by him. Frank had an unconsciously bad habit built into his pitching motion, which Benny would fix through practice. But as for the first game, the damage was done. Frank walked ten batters, and, although we scored nine runs in the game, we were beaten 10–9. Our team was undoubtedly better, and we should never have lost. Although we out-hit and out-fielded the Huntington Park gang, our pitcher and catcher were giving away runs in bunches.

This was not the way an outstanding team planning to win it all should start the season. We were stunned to lose our first game of the season, and we faced the reality that it wasn't going to be as easy as we thought it would be!

Our heads were hanging as we left the field for home. Our confidence had been badly bruised. Benny yelled out to us as he was getting into his car, "Shake it off guys! There are many more games to play. We'll get 'em next time." He wasn't worried, but we sure as hell were!

That tough loss struck our vanity like a chronic case of acne. We couldn't believe we had blown our first game. Joe Maguire made a classic comment that summed it up for all of us, "I can't go home. My dad is going to kill me. Can I sleep overnight with one of you?" We all knew how he was feeling, and we didn't like the way losing hurt our self-esteem. And, boy, did we want to get rid of the pimple-faced impression of being losers.

When we finally released our disappointment about the first game, we focused on not undermining ourselves by playing emotionally and mentally out-of-control baseball. Benny worked with Frank Layana for two days on practicing his delivery motion, making sure that he was bending over properly on the release of his fastball.

"Frank, you're not focusing on your target. Control problems are almost always mental, stemming from a lack of concentration and overthinking."

Frank was a great athlete, but he had tears in his eyes, knowing that his wildness had cost us the game.

"I know, Benny. I'll do better. I promise I'll do better," he said sheepishly, looking away as he tried to hide his tears.

The one-on-one time that Benny spent with Frank would solve the control problems that plagued him in our first game loss. He would never walk that many men in a game again for the remainder of the season.

Following our wake-up call, we moved on to our next

opponent, hoping to demonstrate our new brand of baseball and eager to face the remainder of the season.

Actually, losing the first game of the season was a blessing in disguise, as it proved we were not unbeatable and that every game must be played in a fully conscious state. Our humble beginning woke us up to the fact that if we didn't play as a team and give 100 percent of our effort, we could be beaten any day, no matter how much talent we had amongst us.

Thanks to Benny's Zen master coaching and our strict attention to the mental details of team play, our banded group was unbeatable in our next fifteen games. Even with that one first loss, it was obvious that we were at the top of the Southern California, Los Angeles Area Four Division.

The summer of 1951 was passing quickly, and we won 95 percent of our games by lopsided scores. We lost one more game to a tough Compton team, but we handily won the Los Angeles Area Four Title with twenty-two wins and only two setbacks. The two victories that captured the Area Four title for us were against American Legion Post 508 on July 28 and 29 at Arcadia Park, California. Win number twenty-one was a 7–0 spanking on Saturday, and win number twenty-two was a 7–2 victory on Sunday.

In our first twenty-four games, we had become a well-disciplined, run-scoring machine. We were better coached and more motivated than any other team we had yet faced that summer. But the opposition meter was about to be jacked up a couple of notches because the state playoffs were approaching.

What is the Meaning of Zen?

by

Rafael Espericueta

The word Zen has become part of the English language, but what exactly does it mean? It's much easier to answer the question "*When* is Zen?", for that answer would have to be "Now!". The whole point of Zen practice is to become fully aware, here and now. To come home to the present moment; this is truly where we live. Thinking verbally takes us far into the past, or into the distant future. But both past and future are fantasies, since the future isn't known and our memories of the past are often quite distorted accounts of what really happened. Zen exhorts one to "Come to your senses!", for when we get lost in thoughts of the past or future, life passes us by. When one mindfully dwells in the present moment, one completely dissolves into whatever activity manifests. One becomes the activity. Most people have had peak experiences, which all involve being so totally involved with life that one's sense of separateness dissolves into the experience. Very Zen.

Teenage girls were often intrigued by our practice sessions

10

Carnal Distractions

With the regular season over and the state playoffs around the corner, we had some extra time to hang out at the playground after workouts. This is when girls appeared out of nowhere on the playground to see if they could get us excited about something other than baseball. They knew we would be at the playground all day, and when we weren't working out or playing a game, they would be there to occupy our time. The girls would appear at Rancho with the pretense of playing some of the games that were available around Benny's office. There was ping pong, miniature billiards, checkers, and many more choices. They would challenge us to a game and then tease us with their flirting eyes and sexy, lithe bodies.

The teenage girls who hung out at Rancho knew how to use body language and sultry glances to sexually torment horny teenage boys. They would slink around and "accidentally" rub their supple breasts against us and then say, "Oh, I'm sorry! I didn't mean to do that!"

It was quite exasperating to be seventeen years old with strong pubescent desires and at the same time a baseball player on a winning team with girls hanging around daily. But in 1951, the country wasn't caught up in a rock star mentality, and sex was not loosely engaged in like it is today. Sex was treated as sacred in the 1950s, unlike today. It was an experience you saved for marriage or for a very special person. These days, if you're not having sex by fifteen years old, there is something wrong with you. Sex is a widespread spectator sport with the entire populace competing to see who can "score" the most notches on their bed post. But that sure was not how it was back then.

We had a multitude of innocent activities to help sublimate our desires, baseball being one of them! Yes, we were in the full bloom of adolescence, with hormones erupting out of our skin through a variety of facial blemishes. However, most, if not all, of us were seventeen-year-old virgins eager to become more educated about the sexual domain. We wouldn't be receiving any instruction from our parents or teachers—that was certain.

The ones we turned to for our education were members of our team who had steady girlfriends—George Anderson, Billy Consolo, and Frank Layana. For Billy, the concept of going steady was problematic as he wasn't one to attach himself to any one person or thing. It wasn't clearly apparent that he was actually "going steady," probably due to his Italian upbringing. Italian culture taught us to focus on our mothers and our family ties. Billy was very close to his mother and lived with her until she died.

I can remember being embarrassed about telling my mother that I had a date. It was like I was two-timing her. She demanded to know who the girl was and everything about her. Then there was irritating teasing that lasted for days as my mother and sisters laughed and pointed at me. "Carl's got a girlfriend! Carl's got a girlfriend!" they would chant, laughing at me. I was programmed by my family and the nuns who shamed me into avoiding girls.

It was almost better not to tell them anything and just do it. I'm sure Billy's mother reacted the same way about his dating and going steady with girls. Italian mothers are very possessive of their sons, and Italian fathers are the same about their daughters.

In the 1940s and late into the 1950s, couples "going steady" were not generally having sex. But in the case of my aforementioned teammates, if they were not going there, they were definitely visiting the area.

George and Frank both married their high school sweethearts—both girls named Carol—immediately following graduation. George and Carol Anderson enjoyed fifty-eight years of married bliss. Frank and Carole Layana have been separated for twenty-five years. Consolo never married, the reason being acutely obvious.

The teammates who didn't have steady girlfriends pressed these three guys for details about what it was like dating girls. We were curious and lived our sensual lives vicariously through conversations with these three experienced "ladies' men." They would give us just enough information to pique our interest, without giving up any explicit details. They were not the kiss-and-tell type of guys, although Billy came close with his willingness to give up more information than one needed.

During that summer, Billy Consolo was dating a very sexy girl by the name of Suzy Sorensen, and she was crazy about him. She was the kind of girl you'd expect a baseball star to have—shiny blond hair, perfectly proportioned curves, and a knock-out smile. I also covertly had my eye on her from afar, shyly admiring her blue-eyed good looks and tight body. I loved the way she moved so effortlessly and looked right through you with those piercing blue eyes. She was the type of seductive teenager who could transform a young boy's mind into mush, and I was a willing victim.

I could never compete with Billy for a girl openly, but I would playfully flirt with her when Billy wasn't paying any attention to her. She would flirt back with me but only if Billy was watching her activities. Billy couldn't care less who she was talking to; he wasn't the jealous type. He knew she was his girl for as long as he wanted her. Billy was a very confident, handsome guy and a sports hero at Dorsey High where all the girls attended school. He could date any girl he wanted at Dorsey.

I fantasized about dating Suzy Sorensen every night, but didn't have nearly enough courage to ask her out. I would gaze at her playing ping pong and would focus on her firm breasts as they moved gracefully to and fro with each swing until I couldn't stand it any longer. A little guilt crept into my head from the nuns' instruction about impure thoughts, but it didn't stop me from having them. I was through with the nuns as I was now in high school dealing with the Jesuit priests instead. But the nuns had done their number on me for six years, and I still had the remnants of their brainwashing lingering in my psyche.

The fact that Suzy might be going steady with Billy didn't deter me from having those pesky impure thoughts about her. A double deadly sin, for sure! Many times while in her presence, I couldn't approach her for fear that my fantasies would come out in our conversation.

I'm not sure I would have known what to do or where to go if I had had a date with her. Most guys who dated took their gals to the Leimert Theater, the local movie hangout. They sat in the very back row and "made out" through the whole show.

Once I asked Billy, "Hey, Consie, how did you like the movie?"

He answered with a huge smile on his face, "Who played in it? I never saw a single scene."

Oh, I was so envious of him making out with Suzy. I wanted that job!

What chance did I have for a date with anyone? I was attending an all-boy Catholic high school and had none of the social skills needed to interact with the opposite sex. Not only did I not have a girlfriend, I didn't even have the nerve to approach one. My sex life consisted of a couple of wet dreams a week. Sometimes even the girls in my steamy dreams wouldn't bother showing up for our tryst. Rejection didn't feel pleasant even in my dreams and fantasies.

When we were on the playground and had a break from playing baseball, we would join the girls in their games. The girls would endlessly tease the boys, the real contest being a sensual cat-and-mouse game. The girls were masters of "innocent" sexual undercurrent, which generated a lot of giggling between male and female players. You could easily surmise who was chasing whom, as there wasn't any pretense about it. Many of the girls had methods of stalking their male prey that would make even a lioness proud. The games, while innocent on the surface, reeked of carnality.

I would stare at Suzy and fantasize about what seventeen-year-old boys dream about while engaging in impure thoughts. Once she caught me staring at her and inquired, "What are you looking at?" Suddenly I felt exposed, like I was once again standing in front of the student body in a dress.

I tried to think of some clever retort but drew blanks all around in my mind. I was unaccustomed to matching wits with a sexy, savvy female. She knew I had the hots for her! This gave her even more power to turn up the dial on my already soaring libido. I was overmatched and knew it, so I kept my mouth shut and conceded the contest.

George Anderson's steady girlfriend, Carol Valle, also showed up at the playground to play games and schmooze with the boys. George and Carol had been dating steadily since about the fourth grade, so they were a lock. No one dared mess with Carol, and George didn't dare look at another girl. They were in love and everyone knew it! George said later that he knew in fourth grade that he would eventually marry Carol.

Carol Valle was petite, svelte, and very good looking, and she was an extremely sweet young woman. She was George's girl from day one, and he never let anyone think anything different.

Both George and Carol were straight shooters who didn't play games of the heart. It was obvious they were meant for each other. Carol stuck to George like gum on a shoe, and she loved his cocky self-confidence. It was like she could sense future success in this juvenile delinquent.

Sex and girls were definitely loitering in our brains more than even our parents realized at the time. But make no mistake about it; during the summer, baseball and winning were foremost in our hearts and minds. We were a cohesive group of sixteen bright teenage boys whose energies were synergistically connected by our love of baseball and for each other. Girls, at least while we were playing for the American Legion team, took a back seat to our primary obsession—baseball. We were definitely obsessed with "going all the way," but not in the way kids mean today.

Benny told us, "Girls will always be there for you, but the 16,299 teams in the American Legion system must be disposed of this summer. You can't have both."

Benny rarely mentioned sex or girls in his talks with us unless it was part of a joke. However, he did dwell on our need to stay focused on our goal of winning and blocking out all other distractions. We presumed that included sex and girls. Benny would laughingly say, "Girls and batting averages are alike; they are both only good for show, and they slow you down in the long run."

Benny didn't have much use for batting averages and probably felt the same way about us dating girls. He was a wiz when it came to handling male athletes but didn't seem to have a clue about working with girls. Maybe this was because he was the father of twin boys.

So as far as our team was concerned, girls would be put on the back burner until summer was over and the other teams were no longer standing in our way. After the summer and baseball were over, girls could be permitted back into our brains.

AMERICAN

U·S

LEGION

Joe Maguire, Bill Lachemann, Fred Clampitt,
George Anderson, Frank Layana

11

Whirlwind of Winning

WE WERE NOW UP AGAINST the winners of the San Diego Area Five Division for the Southern California championship, which was to be played in Glendale, California. Our club was pitted against a strong San Diego Post 364 team that dominated their opponents at the south end of the state. The players from San Diego were perfectly matched opponents for our Los Angeles team.

They had power hitting, plenty of speed on the bases, and stingy pitching at that! This would be the first big gut check for us as the California State Playoffs began in August. Were we really as well coached and as motivated as we believed we were? That question would be answered by the end of the weekend.

The first game of a doubleheader had our star athlete, Frank Layana, pitching his heart and arm out for ten and a half innings. However, the game became deadlocked at three runs apiece, each team unwilling to acquiesce. The San Diego team was playing with extreme confidence and was not intimidated by playing in our home park. Their hitting and fielding skills were every bit as accomplished as ours. But Benny had spent many hours preparing our mental toughness for games such as these. Benny gathered us around him in the dugout because he had some advice he wanted to share with his team. "This game is lasting too long and we have another game to play after it, so let's get it over with!"

He talked like we hadn't put in any effort against this tough San Diego team. We looked at each other, thinking, "What does he think we've been trying to do for eleven innings?" Was this another of his head games? Whenever Benny talked to us that way in a game, we knew he wanted us to dig deeper and find a way to win!

Frank Layana, who had pitched brilliantly for eleven innings, was now stepping into the batter's box with the winning run on second base and the chance to end the battle with his bat rather than his arm. As he left the dugout with his bat in hand, he glanced back at us and, without smiling, said, "You guys just sit back and relax because I'm fixin' to end this thing right here and now."

He strode to the plate with perfect confidence, and with two outs he launched a four-hundred-foot triple in the bottom half of the eleventh inning, driving in third baseman Billy Consolo, who had just doubled for his third hit of the day. We had hung on for a hard-fought first game win. We, the Los Angeles Post 715, won the game, 4–3, in eleven tough innings.

As we ran out of the dugout to congratulate Frank, Benny yelled at us, "That's what I'm talkin' about, guys! Now I know you're listening!" Indeed, we were listening and learning what it was like to play Benny Ball!

In the second game of the doubleheader, we thought it would be another tough, close game. But the first heartbreaking game loss in eleven innings took its toll on the athletes from San Diego. They seemed to sleepwalk through the second game. Our shortstop George Anderson's three hits and six RBIs administered the knockout blow that caused their wooziness! And if Anderson's hitting tirade wasn't enough, Billy Consolo had five hits in the two games in eight at bats, and Paul Schulte pitched a six-hit beauty in the second game. In the second game, we overwhelmed and disheartened the San Diego team 13–3 to win both games of the doubleheader.

Now a major validation of our summer of baseball exploits was about to be played out in high drama. The youngsters from La-la Land were on their way to take on the monster from the north. We were challenging Northern California for the coveted California State Championship. Northern California was on a roll, winning the last three years consecutively and winning the national title twice.

The Oakland, California, team was blessed with truly gifted players, including future Hall of Fame inductee Frank Robinson. In 1949, he was a fifteen-year-old starter—at the time the youngest player to start for any team winning an American Legion national championship. Vada Pinson, a future major leaguer, also starred on the team when they won in 1950.

Our 715 Post team traveled to Sacramento in early August on an overnight train leaving from Los Angeles Union Station—a grueling twelve-hour ride. That meant we slept on the train in compartments that paired our players. As you might imagine, getting sixteen hyper youngsters to sleep on a train was quite a chore for Benny Lefebvre. The idea of sleeping in a large moving bedroom was completely foreign to us, and we reacted like the wild group of teenagers that we were.

We were slipping in and out of each other's compartments, playing different versions of grab-ass and harass-your-neighbor. Laughing hysterically and clad in our pajamas, we proceeded to take part in outlandish, youthful hijinks. Benny was losing patience rapidly as he came into our car pleading with us, "You guys get to bed and get some sleep. You're playing a tough team tomorrow night."

But as soon as he left our compartment, we were back at it. Joe Maguire yelled defiantly above the chaos, "We don't need no stinkin' sleep to beat those little shits from Sacramento! All we need to do is show up, and when they see our ugly faces, they'll run for cover!" Everyone laughed wildly and the bedlam continued. Pillows were flying and kids wrestling each other, vying for the right to the top bunk.

Hours later when the impromptu party finally subsided, there were four guys sleeping in one compartment and various numbers sleeping in others. No one got much sleep on that overnight ride, but we had a lot of fun being away from home without parents for the first time! It was like having a team sleepover on wheels. If this was a sample of our conduct on our first night away from home, what could Benny expect in the future? He probably didn't want to think about it!

Upon arriving, a little drowsy, in Northern California, we were opposing a dangerous, heavy-hitting Sacramento team that had top-level pitching and played power baseball. They had only lost three games all year—we had lost only two—and they had awesome numbers to prove the strength of their team. This would be a classic battle between two giants—Sacramento Post 61, Northern California champs, and Crenshaw Post 715, kings of Southern California.

On paper, there was no difference between the two teams. But paper could not record the mental toughness that Benny had instilled in us. It's not something that most people would calculate as an asset for a baseball team, but when things start smoking, it can pull a team's ass out of the fire.

Benny's weird and wonderful brand of baseball had us well prepared for severe baseball action and ready to face harsh treatment from the Sacramento fans who were known for their loud, outlandish style of riding the other team. They didn't hesitate to get downright personal and nasty when facing opposition on the field or at bat.

The two teams gave the Sacramento fans nonstop action that would stimulate their senses and test their nerves that memorable weekend. The fans were given a roller-coaster ride that they would not soon forget!

The opening game, played on a Friday night under the lights, certainly was not a good start for our Los Angeles team. Sacramento lefty Ralph Rose outpitched Layana that night and sent their fans home very happy. This first game was the start of a wild ride for both teams, and even more so for the Sacramento fans. We lost 5–2, despite the fact that Frank Layana pitched well enough to win the game. It was only our third loss of the season, but it appeared that the Northern California team was going to run off with their fourth straight California state title.

Frank Layana on the mound at Sacramento

Our bats went to sleep on a night that we desperately needed alert hitting to compete with Sacramento. It was no wonder after our night of mayhem on the train. We had played that night after arriving that same morning without much sleep. We now were in a deep hole and had to win both games of a doubleheader on Sunday to stay in the national title race.

Sacramento still had to win one more game in a best-of-three series, which would prove to be a difficult task against our determined and very competitive Los Angeles bunch. We were all reminded of our pledge to go all the way on that first day in June. We weren't about to lie down and die because of one game—not for any team. They still had to beat us one more time.

The Sacramento coach had scheduled a doubleheader on Sunday, giving us Saturday off. He probably did this because he only had one good pitcher, lefty Ralph Rose, and wanted to give him an extra day of rest if they needed him on Sunday.

On our day off, we toured the state capitol building and watched a session of the legislature, which nearly bored us to death. The rest of the day we spent hanging out with some schoolmates who had driven up for the weekend series.

Guy Stockwell, a fellow Loyola High student, and his younger brother, Dean, joined us touring the capitol grounds. Later, Guy starred in his own TV series, *Adventures in Paradise*. Dean Stockwell, who later starred in *Quantum Leap*, was a ten-year-old child movie star at the time and was quite content running with some older "men." Although Guy and Dean had plenty of money, we treated them to lunch and dinner.

We relaxed all afternoon, anticipating the uphill battle we had scheduled the next day. We had to win both ends of a doubleheader or we were done for the year. You would never know by our demeanor that we had lost the first game in Sacramento. We were having fun, but the next day would be different. It would be all business!

While we were at the hotel, Benny called a meeting to get us mentally prepared for the difficult doubleheader we had before us. He was serious about what his expectations were for our team.

He addressed us in his usual Zen-like fashion: "Guys, playing winning baseball is like turning on a light switch. When it's on, you're playing good baseball. When it's turned off, you're playing losing baseball. During a game, if you turn off the switch, you can't turn it back on. The switch must be left on the whole game. Let me explain. When the switch is on, you are conscious. You're concentrating on every pitch and every play. You know what your job is, and you execute it the way you've been taught. When the switch is off, your head is not in the game. You're thinking about something else, and it's not baseball. When you think about something else, you make mental mistakes that cost us games. That's what happened Friday night. You guys were not playing fully conscious in that game. You were somewhere else."

He looked around at us to see if he had lost any of us. We were sure we knew where he was headed with his latest baseball riddle. We were also learning to think like a Zen master—outside the box.

"Are you with me so far?" We all nodded in agreement

"Remember, like I said before, the key is keeping the light switch on at all times during the game. If it's turned off, it can't be turned back on. So when I tell you individually or as a team to turn on your switch, what message am I sending you? Georgie?"

George Anderson was listening intently and wasn't caught off-guard. He knew the answer to the question and couldn't wait to respond to it.

"It means to pull our heads out of our butts and wake up!" Everyone laughed and Benny nodded. "That's close enough," he said.

"Tomorrow we play two games, and I want the light turned on for both games. I don't want you to turn it off, even between games. Do you get me? I want the light switch turned on all day, and the light has to be blindingly bright!"

We all smiled and that told him that we were all on the same page. We had clearly understood his message. We were finally all speaking the same language.

On a bright, hot, and humid Sunday morning in Sacramento, a doubleheader, if needed, was scheduled to determine which team was leaving California and traveling southeast to Winslow, Arizona, for the regional playoffs. The day turned out to be a very long, nerve-wracking battle between two very good teams, each refusing to accept defeat that day.

The first game was a never-ending seesaw struggle; each team scored multiple runs, which were assisted by twenty-nine walks in the game. Our team started the scoring in the bottom of the first inning with four runs and felt good about our chances, but it was way too early to get comfortable with a small lead. The lead changed hands almost every inning with runs being scored and with many pitching changes causing delays in an already long game. The crowd was boisterous and, of course, highly biased toward Sacramento. White towels were waved, and devoted, screaming fans created a cacophony that far exceeded what would be expected from the relatively small gathering of the 3,500 loyal Sacramento followers. They were intent on cheering their team to the state championship, so they tried to unnerve us with loud personal slurs. Even ethnic slurs were fair game for that fanatical Sacramento crowd.

They yelled out, "Go home, kikes and wops!" whenever one of our Jewish or Italian players was hitting at home plate. Billy Consolo and I, being of Italian descent, put our heads together and came up with a plan.

"The only way to shut these assholes up is to beat the shit out of 'em." Being called a wop made Billy's blood boil!

I said in response, "Okay, Billy, great plan. Now let's make it happen so we can go home with the championship."

The Sacramento fans had pissed us off, and their unsportsmanlike words only motivated us to engage in a fiercer battle with their team. I don't think that the overzealous Sacramento fans realized their unsavory behavior was actually hurting their team, not helping them. I felt sorry for the Sacramento players. They weren't aware that their redneck supporters were supplying us with all the motivation we needed to win the game. Their biggest blunder was creating anger in Billy's psyche.

Benny had taught us well to be mentally resilient. He would say, "When things on the field get rough, don't react with emotion. Instead, respond with your instincts." When we responded on the field with our instincts, it took our minds out of the equation. "The chief enemy to succeeding in baseball is thinking too much," Benny often told us.

"Don't let thinking get in the way of being a good ballplayer."

Our confidence took a dive as our early innings lead vanished, and we were down 9–6 after six innings. However, the seventh inning proved to be lucky for us. I started the inning by being hit by a pitch, and then southpaw Ralph Rose loaded the bases by walking both Jerry Siegert and Mel Goldberg. With two outs, Joe Maguire singled me home for one run. The next batter was the man who wanted to shut the pie-holes of the bigoted Sacramento fans—Billy Consolo, also known as Superman. Now he had his light switch on and shining bright!

Billy ripped a Ralph Rose pitch for a long drive to left center field, and it rattled off the left field wall, bouncing away from the fielders. After all the commotion and dust settled, Billy was standing on third base, and we were leading in the game 10–9! The fans had tugged on Superman's cape and that wasn't very smart.

Our lead in the seventh inning incited the obnoxious Sacramento fans to a new level of noise, ethnic abuse, and towel-waving to distract us. But the home fans' loudmouth antics didn't work for their team. We, the "good guys" of Post 715, won game one of the doubleheader in a wild and crazy tug-of-war that resulted in a 10–9 victory. When the bizarre contest was over, four of our players, Paul Schulte, Billy Consolo, Don Kenway, and Frank Layana, had made an effort pitching in that game. They allowed sixteen walks, but only three earned runs. After all that, Frank Layana was the winning pitcher.

The score did not indicate the intense effort that both teams and fans put forth to produce this epic battle. Either team could have won as each had many opportunities to do so. But our team desired it the most! We switched our lights on and proved we had the discipline to play hard in close games!

Now we were playing the rubber match to see who would go home and who would continue toward the ultimate prize that waited in Detroit, Michigan. It was obvious that the winner of this one game would be favored to win it all. Both teams were capable of running the table if they won this one contest. The intensity of the crowd noise increased by many decibels and the pressure began to show on the faces of the ballplayers. This was it! The whole season was wrapped up in this one game of winner-takes-all California State Championship.

Between games, Benny kept our light beams switched on high with talk of this being our National Championship game, even though we were really playing for the California State Title. His confidence and enthusiasm were contagious, and our lights grew brighter and brighter!

If anyone thought the first game was exciting, little did they know that they were in for an even more intense battle in the final game. The rubber match was the complete antithesis of the first game of the day. This was a tight game played with high precision, with few mistakes on either side. The pitchers for the deciding game were none other than Ralph Rose and Frank Layana, the same throwers who had bumped heads Friday night. Also, both athletes had pitched some innings in the first game of the double-header. However, Ralph Rose had absorbed his first loss of the series when he gave up the winning run of the day's first game.

Sacramento scored two runs on three hits in the second inning to take a two-run lead. One run was scored on a single by Jim Fellos and another run came in on an error by our shortstop George "Sparky" Anderson. In the sixth inning Billy Consolo walked, stole second base, and then scored on a solid single by Bill Lachemann. The score after six innings was Sacramento 2, Los Angeles 1.

In the top of the seventh inning Don Kenway opened with a single, followed by my hit to right field. Then the third batter Mel Goldberg continued the trend with a sharp single to right field, allowing Kenway to score from second. With the score tied at 2–2 and two outs with the bases loaded, lefty Ralph Rose walked Frank Layana and forced in what would prove to be the winning run. Ralph Rose, Sacramento's star pitcher, had won the first game on Friday night then proceeded to lose both ends of the double-header on Sunday. Talk about going through your extreme highs and lows in one weekend! It was another hard fought war, a flip-of-the-coin game that could have gone either way. But the flip of the coin turned up heads for the boys with the laser bright light switches!

By the end of the day both teams were totally exhausted—physically, mentally, and emotionally—and the Sacramento fans were hoarse and silent at last. As the teams shook hands at the end of the longest day of their lives, the ones with slight grins on their faces were wearing the Los Angeles uniforms. The boys of Los Angeles Post 715, in an epic cat fight, had out scratched the guys from Sacramento Post 61 with a final score of 3–2. Our mental toughness had paid off, winning us the doubleheader by just one run in each game.

Both winning and losing teams left every last ounce of valor on the field and were happy not to encounter each other again. After the three-game series, only one run separated the two teams. Oddly enough, the team with the most runs lost the California State Championship. No wonder they had tears streaming down their faces when their highly successful season came to an abrupt halt, thanks to the party crashers from the City of the Stars.

Frank Layana and Billy Consolo were the co-heroes of the series—Billy with his timely power hitting and Frank with his superior pitching velocity and endurance. Out of the twenty-eight innings in the three games performed, Frank had pitched twenty-one of them with a 0.79 ERA. Talk about carrying a team on your back! Frank Layana had done just that! He also carried the Player of the Series honor back home with him to Los Angeles.

That night we celebrated our hard-won state championship at

our hotel by throwing water bombs out the ninth-floor windows onto unsuspecting pedestrians below. Bobby Morris came running into the room I shared with Frank Layana. He was laughing and bellowing, "I got one! I got a guy right on his left shoulder, and he didn't know what hit him!"

A little concerned, I queried, "Is he okay? I mean, was he hurt?"

A water balloon dropped from nine stories high could hit with the impact of a sledgehammer. Bobby answered before I could even finish, "Nah, no, he's fine. He's trying to find out where it came from, but he's fine."

Bobby's face showed anxiety about possibly getting into trouble over the incident since he wasn't actually trying to hit anyone. It's hard to hit anything with a water balloon from almost one hundred feet off the ground. It was purely a lucky hit, but not for the guy who received it.

This rowdy behavior would set the tone for our team throughout the remainder of the long season. The hotel investigated complaints about the water bombs, but they couldn't pinpoint the exact room from which the wet missiles had emanated. So we were let off the hook and dodged our first bullet off the field. But there were plenty more to come. We were well-meaning kids with too much exuberance and idle time in our daily baseball schedule.

Later, we celebrated our victory by ordering food from room service and having a party in George and Billy's room. We played cards, sang, and ate junk food. Of course, Billy told jokes and entertained us as we laughed the night away.

One of Billy's jokes started, "This slimy Sacramento fan slithers into a bar." He wiggled his hand to indicate the movement of a snake. That was all he needed to say! We started to laugh and didn't stop for ten minutes. He kept up with the stand-up comedy act until we were doubled over and lying on the floor.

No one slept a wink that night, even though we were dead tired from the two stressful games we had battled through that long day. Our light switches were still turned to high beam, I guess!

We were very thankful to have those three games behind us and to come out of it victorious against the best team we were likely to face all year. We also knew that after you win in California, the competition drops off considerably. A California team had won the National Title two years in a row.

Getting on the train back to Los Angeles the next day, we felt highly confident about our chances of winning it all. We weren't overly cocky, but we were feeling extremely self-assured. Halfway home, we ran through the train, waving our newly won trophies and chanting, "LA RULES! SACRAMENTO DROOLS!" I felt satisfied that I had contributed a lot to our victories in Sacramento, and the fact that the bigoted Sacramento fans went home depressed gave me another kind of satisfaction!

Just outside of Los Angeles, George Anderson sat down next to me and said, "Ya know, Mag, I now think that we really do have a chance of winning this whole dang thing."

My reply was, "Georgie, we're only halfway there, but I also feel real good about our destiny."

We both agreed that after coming back from our first loss and winning the very close doubleheader, we were more than ready for baseball outside of California.

There were photographers and reporters waiting for us when we arrived at the Union Train Station in Los Angeles. They surrounded our coach, Benny Lefebvre, asking questions about the doubleheader win in Sacramento. Then they lined up the team for some pictures, and now we really thought we were hot stuff. Remember, we were just seventeen years old and had never had this much attention in our entire lives.

While we were lined up for a picture, Benny smiled and said, "If you like winning, smile!"

He had programmed our expanding brains to crave winning! He never stopped talking about winning! Every other sentence had the "W" word in it! Benny believed that if you thought like a winner, acted like a winner, and talked like a winner, then you would become a winner. Winning was a matter of convincing your brain that you could and would win! Was it mind over matter? Whatever it was, Benny knew exactly what he was doing—using his subliminal skills of persuasion to motivate us to play at the apex of our abilities. With Benny subtly targeting our short attention spans and softly pushing us, we were flying high!

The next week was spent getting sponsorships to support our trip to our first stop—Winslow, Arizona—for the Region 12 American Legion Junior Baseball Tournament. The Winslow tournament was the first of three we had to win to become national champs. There were four teams, including us, in the tournament in Winslow. The teams were from Tucson, Arizona; Reno, Nevada; Farmington, Utah; and the land of hot shot troublemakers—Los Angeles, California.

Before we left for Arizona, we secured a DeSoto-Plymouth dealership in Los Angeles by the name of Marshall-Clampitt as our financial sponsor, which ended up being one the best things that happened to us money-wise. Each player was given five dollars per diem for meal money. That was a lot of money at that time, considering that a loaf of bread cost fifteen cents and a dozen eggs cost less than twenty cents. Back then, you could have a quality three-course dinner for around two dollars.

On payday, Benny lined us up and announced, "Every three days you will each receive fifteen dollars for food money, and if you run out of money before the next payday, don't come looking for me." We thought, "How could anyone eat that much food?" as we reached out for the three five dollar bills.

George Anderson stuffed the cash in his pocket and whispered while licking his lips, "Boy, am I gonna have fun with this windfall."

George came from a poor family, so that was probably more money than he had ever felt in his hands at one time. We would observe on our next road trip just how wisely George spent his meal money.

We found out later, when Billy Consolo went to the big leagues, those major league players were getting seven dollars per diem. So we were living high off our sponsor with cash bulging out of our pockets, enabling us to eat like high rollers. The five dollars a day began adding up since we couldn't eat that much food in a day, so the money started growing. The cash that was left over after eating was spent mostly on entertainment and gifts for our families.

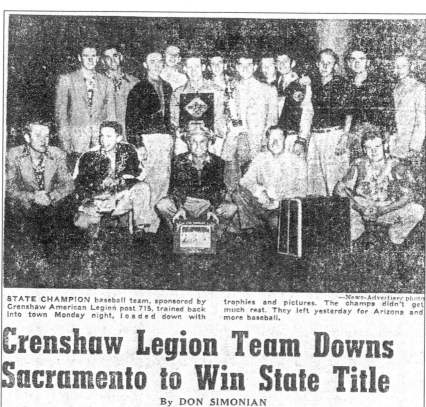

—News-Advertiser photo

STATE CHAMPION baseball team, sponsored by Crenshaw American Legion post 715, trained back into town Monday night, loaded down with trophies and pictures. The champs didn't get much rest. They left yesterday for Arizona and more baseball.

Crenshaw Legion Team Downs Sacramento to Win State Title

By DON SIMONIAN

Bringing to a close the supremacy of northern California Legion basebal squads, the Crenshaw post 715 American Legion nine proved victorious last weekend

American Legion
Junior Baseball Tournament

REGION 12

WINSLOW, ARIZONA, AUGUST 18-21, 1951

Roster of Teams and Officials

ARIZONA
(Morgan McDermott Post No. 7, Tucson)

No.		Pos.
2	Glen Festin	C
12	Ricardo Manzo	C
1	Albert Gallego	P
11	Arthur Halverson	P
18	Burt Kinerk	P
5	Thomas Scott	P
14	Henry Ybarra	P
3	Donald Poorman	1B
4	Thomas Tellez	2B
6	Donald Swaim	SS
10	William Codd	3B
7	Pat Pate	LF
8	Lee Myers	CF
9	Earl Jackson	RF
16	Guy Barickman	U
17	Thomas Flood	U
20	Chuck Hollinger	Coach

Joe Hanson, Manager

NEVADA
(Darrell Dunble Post No. 1, Reno)

11	Frank O. Ames	C
6	Howard F. Seeman	C
16	Don P. Clark	OF
12	Ken Fujil	C
9	Lester L. Mack	P & OF
17	Roger S. Trounday	SS
5	Bill B. Jessup	OF
14	Ron W. Hart	OF
10	George W. Smith	OF
33	Rudy Galli	1B
7	Henry de Ircco	2B
15	Don Bissett	OF
4	Robert A. Neal	3B
30	Dan Hellman	P
8	Ken Cerica	OF
16	Dick Snyder	P & OF

Ray Ward, Jr., Coach
Buddy Garfinth, Manager

CALIFORNIA
(Marshall-Clampitt, DeSoto-Plymouth)
(Crenshaw Post No. 715, Los Angeles)

No.		Pos.
10	Bill Consolo (C)	3B
17	Frank Layana	P
11	Joe Maguire	2B
	Bill Lachemann	C
15	George Anderson (CO-C)	SS
8	Mel Goldberg	IF
3	Carl Maggio	RF
7	Bob Morris	CF
	Paul Schulte	P
	Warren Johnson	IF
14	Don Kenway	LF
3	Guy McElwaine	P
	Jerry Seigert	1B
	Gordon Sherett	OF
4	Warren Appley	OF
	Wilford Zander	P
	Benny LeFebvre	Coach

Charles Wilson, Manager

UTAH
(Farmington Post No. 27, Farmington)

Lynn H. Burningham	P & OF
Billie Gene Bell	OF & 1B
Ronald H. Smith	3B
Bill Workman	P
Weldan Hamblin	P
Don A. Stringham	C
Finly Hansen	C
Carl Vernon Clayton	2B
Vlado Joe Lopez	SS
Douglas Jensen	1B
Clark Draayer	1B & OF
Max Elliott	2B & OF
Norman Elliott	OF
Elmer Brambaugh	3B & OF

Edwin Earle, Coach
Arthur D. Miller, Manager

THE CODE OF SPORTSMANSHIP

Keep the rules.
Keep faith with your comrades.
Keep your temper.
Keep yourself fit.
Keep a stout heart in defeat.
Keep your pride under in victory.
Keep a sound soul, a clean mind and a healthy body.

12

Giving It Up for the Team

On the night of August 16, 1951, we boarded the train again. This time going east, in the direction of our dreams—Detroit, Michigan. But first we had to take care of business in between trip stops, and our first business trip was scheduled for Winslow, Arizona, with a population of about nine thousand.

After our previous sleepy performance in Sacramento, we were finished with hijinks on overnight train rides. We knew that we needed to get a good night's sleep during the long train ride to Winslow. We awoke the next morning to the sight of dense, picturesque pine trees outside the train's windows as we passed through Flagstaff, Arizona, still an hour away from Winslow. Would Winslow be as scenic as Flagstaff? We were hoping it would be green and cool. Instead we found a little town in the middle of a flat, dry desert.

Winslow was a small town built by the Santa Fe Railroad in the middle of a Navajo reservation in Northern Arizona. Few had ever heard of it until it achieved national fame in 1972. A rock group called the Eagles had a huge hit song called "Take It Easy," which included prominent lyrics about the town: "Standing on the corner in Winslow, Arizona, such a fine sight to see." That song would put Winslow on the map.

In those days, if you didn't work for the railroad or a related industry, you had no business being there. There was absolutely nothing to do in the town for sixteen teenage boys who were away from home and desperately seeking some excitement. We also had money burning holes in our pockets with no place to spend it!

The township was a truck stop on Route 66, which was the only two-lane road at the time that connected Chicago with the West Coast. Most people traveling east or west stopped there for gas. Few travelers spent the night in Winslow because there wasn't a decent hotel or motel there at the time and the nearby city of Flagstaff had more to offer its visitors. In the 1970s, Winslow was bypassed by I-40, a new four-lane freeway that also went on to Chicago.

Upon arriving around noon, we checked into our dumpy hotel, which was less than second class. It didn't look like a hotel, and it didn't smell like one either. It was a square box with no redeeming architectural features and no curb appeal whatsoever. It had no sign on the building identifying what its purpose was, and it appeared to have been abandoned by the world. It resembled a flophouse, and from the outside you couldn't see through the dirty windows. To make things worse, there was no air conditioning in the rooms, except in the hallways. It was August in Arizona, which meant the outside temperatures were in excess of 105 degrees. Inside the hotel, it felt even warmer, and it was difficult to sleep while lying in a pool of your own sweat.

The governor of Arizona, Howard Pyle, was in Winslow to throw out the first ball in the first game between Utah and Arizona. The tournament was the third regional meeting held in Winslow in as many years. It was expertly conducted under the general leadership of chairman Bus Mead, past Department Commander for Arizona. His organizational skills were unparalleled in the

American Legion, which made his baseball tournaments some of the best in the nation.

Our California contingent met Bus Mead and his daughter Pattie at the inaugural Legion Party held for all the four teams playing in Winslow. Pattie Mead had accompanied her father to the event as an unpaid helper and probably to meet some of the baseball guys. We didn't mind her looking at us because we didn't mind looking at her. She was a pretty young thing with light brown hair and a round, cheerful face. She wore a sleeveless pink sundress that showed off her sun-kissed bronze skin.

The moment I met her, Pattie became the focal point of my attention during our stay in Winslow. Upon shaking her hand, my eyes locked onto her welcoming blue eyes and I wanted to get to know her better. To my good fortune, she felt the same way about me, and she asked me, "What are you doing after the party tonight?"

I surprised myself with my answer: "Whatever you want to do!"

Her smile exposed perfectly white, pearl-like teeth matching a very pretty face. I was swiftly smitten with her, and she had me under her magical teenage charm.

"I have a car. We can go for a ride and talk." The way she said the word talk, I could tell she intended something other than captivating conversation. I was excited and nervous because we had a curfew of 10:00 PM, and it was already 8:00 PM.

I stuttered momentarily but got it out. "P-p-pick me up in front of my hotel in ten minutes."

I grinned at her, then turned and walked out of the party with my heart pounding briskly in my chest. I walked five blocks to my hotel, about five minutes away, to find her in her dad's Chevy Suburban waiting in front of the hotel. My mind raced, "How did she do that so fast?"

I slithered into the passenger's seat without breaking stride, and off we went into the darkening desert. She made some small talk while she headed for a quiet place to park her Suburban.

"How do you like living in California?" she asked. I was hyperventilating and sounded like I had just run a mile.

"It's okay. Just like … any big … city … I guess." Sweat was running down my forehead, and I felt like my heart was going to explode with her sitting next to me.

She turned to me and asked, "Are you okay? I mean, you sound out of breath."

I nodded that I was fine but didn't speak. I smiled sheepishly at her, took a deep breath, and tried to regain my composure.

She continued, "Living anywhere would be better than this boring desert sand trap."

She steered the Suburban into a deserted parking lot, found a place to park, and cut her lights. The sun had dropped below the horizon and the temperature was finally dropping.

"Let's get into the back seat. There is more room back there."

Her vehicle had three rows of seats, and in the back row there was much more room for whatever we had on the menu. We climbed into the back seat, and she promptly lay down on the back seat facing me. I froze for a moment, shocked by her unexpected, aggressive move, I felt my knees get weak and buckle. The next thing I knew, I was kneeling by her side, leaning over her with my eyes transfixed by hers. As if moving on their own, my hands slid up her arms and up behind her shoulders.

We embraced and kissed sweetly at first, and then passionately, until we had to back off and take some time to breathe. We were getting too hot and heavy and needed to come up for air. She was about sixteen years old and experienced at kissing, which made it very enjoyable for me because I loved kissing her.

She was truly a sweet sixteen beauty, and I felt warm in her embrace. It was dark out, but the temperature was still fairly warm. Who knows how many degrees were added by her firm clasp around my neck. Pattie's hand slid onto mine. She grasped my hand

and guided it toward her breast. The surprise threw me off my game as I was strictly a singles hitter not familiar with second base. But it appeared Pattie was urging me to steal second. Impure thoughts began to pour into my head. Damn those nuns! She offered me the steal signal then second base was taken without a throw.

We kissed and petted lightly for about an hour until I grasped it was past the team's curfew, the bewitching hour. Cinderella was already fifteen minutes past being turned into a pumpkin, and twenty minutes from being tucked into bed by the mice. I was in a conundrum. I didn't want to leave, I was sweating bullets, and it wasn't because of the desert climate; it was this appealingly carnal schoolgirl next to me.

"Look at the time, Pattie. Oh my God!" I yelled, jumping up, staring at my watch aided by the moonlight, "I've got to get back. I've got a game tomorrow and the coach will be making bed checks. It's ten fifteen already."

She knew I didn't want to leave, but she also felt that she didn't want to be the cause of my getting into trouble. After a few more delicious kisses, we worked our way back into the front seat and headed toward the hotel. She stopped and let me out on a side street, a short distance from the hotel.

As I hustled out of the car, she said, "It was fun; maybe we can do something together again tomorrow?"

Feeling anxious about being late for lockdown, I answered, "Why don't you come out to our game tomorrow night at Vargas Field?"

"Great! I'll see you there, and after you play your game, then we can play!" She smiled slyly and waved as she drove away.

I was a jumble of emotions and couldn't think straight, so I waved good-bye and ran into the hotel lobby up the stairs to my room. I was in a rush to be inside my room in the event there was a bed check. I didn't want to get caught being late for a room inspection the first night on the road. Benny would not be happy with me and would probably sit me on the bench for a game.

As I burst into my room, my roommate, Frank Layana, was writing a letter to his girlfriend with a mischievous grin on his face.

"Where in the hell have you been? Benny was here looking for you and was pissed."

My heart practically stopped beating. I was in deep distress!

"Ooh, shit! I'm screwed! How long ago did he leave here?"

"About two minutes ago, and as he left he said something about getting you a bus ticket back to…"

As my pulse was pounding, I moved closer to Frank to hear the remainder of his statement, but he never finished it.

Frank couldn't keep up the charade any longer. He burst into laughter. Pointing at me, he howled, "Man, I had your ass burning! You should have seen the look on your Italian puss!"

I should have known better. Frank Layana was a notorious practical joker, and he had seized the moment with his impeccable timing. He had nailed my ass. As perfectly as the prank was executed, and as much fun as it was for him, I wanted to kill him.

However, he was much bigger and stronger than I was, so that was out of the question. I loved Frank as I loved all my teammates, but he had an irritating way of getting your goat. He definitely had the nasty gene somewhere in his DNA, and, being his roommate, I was receiving the full brunt of it.

After I calmed down from my near heart attack, I lay in bed thinking about the time I had spent with Pattie in the backseat of the Suburban. I had savored it immensely. Actually, I had enjoyed it a little too much and wanted more! It was like my impure thoughts had come to fruition, and I wanted to act on them. Conflictingly, I felt a little guilty about being the only team member going out with a girl when we were supposed to be concentrating on baseball.

What if all the other guys were also messing around with cuties and missed curfew because of it? That would be a significant disruption for the team as a whole and everything Benny preached against!

I remembered Benny emphasizing in one of our meetings, "When one member of the team chooses to use his power of free will in ways that do not reflect the higher good of the group, then the whole unit suffers."

That was exactly what I was doing, so I then made the difficult decision to withdraw from my rendezvous with Pattie the following night.

As much as I wanted to be with Pattie again, I realized that I was there to play baseball and be an integral part of a winning team. I had thought about it long and hard and believed I made the correct decision. I was giving it up for the good of the team. Pattie Mead would be a major distraction—a pleasurable one, but still a diversion—that would cause me to feel irresponsible as a team member. Was I being foolish? Not if you asked the nuns! At the end of that day I was still a team member and still a virgin. There was nothing in the near future that would change either.

We had our first game scheduled with the Tucson team the next night on August 18, 1951. But some strange things happened on the way to our first encounter outside of California. It seemed that having some money in our pockets and being away from home for the first time inspired weird things to happen to some of us.

On the morning of our night game, a group of us went out to breakfast without any adults. Most of us ordered bacon and eggs or hotcakes. But George Anderson fulfilled a lifelong ambition by drinking a vanilla milkshake for breakfast. His parents were notoriously strict, so he had probably never had the chance to choose his own breakfast. Being away from their influence and having a pocket full of money, he was going for it. When that shake went down effortlessly, the waitress returned and he ordered another. This one was strawberry that he said tasted really silky smooth, "the best breakfast ever." While we ate our boring breakfasts, we all watched him intently as he savored the last drop of his weird breakfast and wondered what this guy with too much money would do next. Then he summoned the waitress requesting a third one—chocolate, of course. The waitress was giddy with surprise as she fought back her motherly instinct to say, "Enough!" He didn't just consume the three milkshakes, he inhaled them. Before he finished one shake, he was looking for a sequel. Billy Consolo topped breakfast off by asking, "What are you having for dessert? A ham sandwich?"

After breakfast, as we walked back to the hotel, George had a self-righteous, milkshake grin on his face. His stomach had popped out noticeably, but he had fulfilled a boyhood fantasy. We asked him how he enjoyed his exotic breakfast. "Deeelicious!" he replied with a broad grin on his face as he tried to hold back a gleeful belly laugh.

We were all a little envious of his triple-shake breakfast orgy, even though we didn't have the courage to go there. His breakfast had cost him 75 cents and ours cost us $1.25, so he was quite proud of his own frugality, at least for the moment.

When we returned to the hotel around noon, we relaxed and rested up for the game. Those of us with excess energy went looking for some lighthearted prankish action. After a couple hours of trying to nap in the sweltering hotel and pulling some mischievous tricks, the word spread throughout the team that one of our players was very sick.

Guess who? Right! It was our star shortstop, the triple-shake guy, and it would take a miracle that night for George to be available to contribute in our game. How could we have such bad luck? Our first day away from home, one of our key players fell ill. Not a good sign for our future. No one seemed to realize that he had simply overdosed on lactose. It wasn't a case of bad luck so much as bad breakfast choices.

Some of us visited him and found the coach and manager there, trying to comfort a player who had earlier sucked up three shakes and was now vomiting profusely. We tried talking to him while he lay on his bed moaning, but he was too sick to respond to us. He didn't stay very long on the bed, as he rushed to the toilet to deliver more rainbow milk shake deposits. After a while, he just sat on the floor next to the bowl with his head hanging over the edge. I had a vision of us playing that night without George at shortstop because it was clear that he would be hugging that toilet for some time.

I was getting queasy just watching him, and I wasn't sure that what he had wasn't contagious. I loved Georgie, and my heart ached for him and shared his nausea, a condition I had experienced so many times. I couldn't watch anymore. I left the room with him hanging his head over the commode, knowing he wasn't nearly finished filling the toilet with breakfast.

Upon seeing the condition he was in, it seemed impossible that George would be playing shortstop that night. We were depressed about not having our popular teammate joining us for the opening game. He was an All-City selection with all the baseball tools necessary, not to mention that he was the sparkplug of our team—maybe the reason he later got the nickname "Sparky." He had upchucked for the better part of three hours and looked like he was ready to be buried in the Arizona desert.

We all knew that George was a tough warrior and could handle himself in any combative situation. He was known in the neighborhood as a likable kid with a dysfunctional temper. Looking at him many "tough guys" thought they could take him in a fight. He was smallish but hard as core steel and what they didn't know was he had a tenacious will that would never quit or give up. He didn't start fights but he sure could finish them. He didn't walk around like a tough guy with a chip on his shoulder, but he feared no one. Most of the time, he sported a black eye proving he could take a beating as well as dish it out. Yes, he was a fighter, but that night he had an invisible opponent that would be difficult to overcome. In this struggle George was overmatched … or was he?

We didn't know how much of a challenge this Tucson team was going to be for us, and we didn't know if we could win without George since he had played shortstop in every inning of every game all summer long. Traveling to the ballpark on the bus, we braced ourselves for the worst case scenario. We all wondered who was penciled in to play shortstop. No one else on the team had played the position all summer.

It was a question, as it turned out, that didn't need an answer. George had no intention of reneging on his role in that game. He sat at the end of the bench until game time, looking like a frozen seated corpse with his face as white as a sheet. About five minutes before the umpire called, "Play ball!" Benny walked over to him to ask the obligatory question, thinking he knew the answer.

"How do you feel, son?" Benny queried.

"I've felt better, but I'll tell you one thing, Benny; I'm playing tonight!" George gasped.

Benny stood there in utter disbelief; he had stayed with George most of the day and witnessed the ordeal he had been through. "I think you should rest this ..." George interrupted, looking into Benny's eyes, "I'm playing tonight, Benny!"

The umpire interrupted Benny's plea by yelling, "Play ball!"

George jumped off the bench and moved swiftly past Benny and onto the field before he could get out another utterance.

As the team took the field for the start of the game, we were flabbergasted to see George standing at shortstop. It was a miracle! The lifeless body of our shortstop had been resurrected. Within minutes his color returned and the spark was back in his body. Billy eyeballed him from third base dumbfounded, "Well, you little sumbich, I never thought I'd see you out here tonight."

"You don't think I'd sit on the bench and watch you have all the fun, do ya?" George replied, forcing a weak grin.

The guys on the team were troubled regarding George's condition, seeing him on the field after what he had been through earlier. We rolled our eyes in skepticism as if to say, "Yeah, right!

Quit with the jokes already!" This was no joke because no one was laughing!

George played that night, and what a brilliant performance he put on! It would have stood as outstanding handiwork for a healthy person, but for an individual who had been vomiting all day, it was beyond belief! He had three hits in five times at bat. He scored three runs and fielded his position with a couple of great plays that I had never seen him execute before.

Except for three different colored milk shakes, which he no longer possessed, he hadn't eaten all day. I'll never know where he got the energy to play that entire contest. That day he got my vote for MVP of the game, although no such vote was ever taken. That night he had my vote for president of the world, even though I was too young to vote at the time. We were trained by Benny to compete mentally and physically, and in just one game, George defined those terms for us.

As if the game wasn't surreal enough with George's super-human effort, a monsoon rain and wind storm appeared out of nowhere and the game was delayed for about an hour or so. Dark clouds turned to black, as wind gusts blew dust up into the air, making it impossible to see the dirt field from the dugout. The thunder and lightning put on quite a show, and then the rain came, quick and hard, and then exited just as rapidly. It was a spectacle that we, of California breed, had never witnessed!

Initially worried that George might be dead weight once the game started, we all felt that we had to step up and put out more force. Everyone on the team was highly productive that night, and no one was surprised when Consolo overpowered a ball that departed the stadium and never seemed to land in the state of Arizona. It skyrocketed off his bat, soaring into the night and disappearing somewhere between Winslow and Flagstaff. With Pattie Mead watching in the stands, I got three hits and was happy to have her there viewing my performance. Unfortunately, we didn't celebrate together after the game, and she fully understood why. We waved to each other after the game with knowing gazes that said, "Maybe a different time, maybe another place … maybe?"

We rolled over Tucson with a lopsided, football-style score of 27–6, and at that point there was no doubt who was the team to beat in the Winslow tournament.

If we hadn't already known by then, we all learned that night about the value of our great shortstop. Never, ever count George Anderson out of anything that had to do with competition or winning! He played the game of baseball as a winner his whole life. That day in Winslow, Arizona, was the day I knew this young man had the fortitude and intelligence to do something significant with his life in the sport of baseball.

He was eventually inducted into the Baseball Hall of Fame in August of 2000 in Cooperstown, New York, after his playing and managing days were over. And, to no one's surprise, he was voted in on the first ballot on which he was eligible for election. A large contingent of teammates and friends, of which I was one, were on hand to commemorate and honor his passage into baseball immortality.

Whenever I tell this story, I end it by saying, "If there were a Hall of Fame for being an exceptional human being, George Anderson would be the first one in it." This man has set a great example for every young baseball player growing up and playing baseball on the playgrounds of every city in this great country. For all the levels of achievement he has earned in his life and baseball career, he is by far the most humble, honest, and authentic human being that I have ever met!

In the sixty-five years that I knew George, I never heard him utter a spiteful or mean word about anyone. Many times while the team was in Sedona for our reunion, and we were eating in a local restaurant, people would come up to him, interrupting our dinner for an autograph. He would drop what he was eating and not only sign an autograph, but talk to them for ten minutes. After going back to his cold dinner, he would say with a mouth full of food, "I love people. I love talking to people from all over the world. I never get tired of it!"

He learned a valuable lesson from his father, who told him as a young boy, "Georgie, it doesn't cost you one thin dime to be nice and respectful to other people."

His father was not a rich man, but the life lessons he conferred upon his son were priceless. George heeded his father's counsel every day he lived. Until the day he died in May of 1985, George's dad was very proud of his son.

After that game our team acquired a deep understanding of the word *courage*. After George played half dead, no one on the team would complain about sore arms, pulled hamstrings, or any other annoying ache or pain. We played through any and all injuries out of respect for the grit he displayed that night in Winslow. I believe that what went on in the first game in Winslow, with George's spunk and strength of character, set the example for mental toughness that Benny was trying to teach us. We had seen with our own eyes a member of our team perform an act of incredible mental and physical toughness. Wow! George was a perfect example of a player who knew how to give it up for the team!

The competition in Winslow was not up to the standards we had encountered in California, so we coasted to consecutive victories against Farmington, Utah, 7–2 and again beat Tucson, Arizona, 11–0. The games were not very exciting because we dominated the teams from the smaller states. The rumors that we had heard were true; after leaving California the competition declined significantly. With the huge population in California and the year-round sunshine, it was a hotbed for baseball talent.

With no competition from the other teams and the pressure off, I contemplated hooking back up with Pattie Mead. As much as I would have liked to be with her again, I thought better of it and stayed away. I still think about her and wonder what she is up to these days.

Most of the excitement was off the playing field, where our players were becoming restless with too much idle time on our hands. Because the heat in Arizona was so unbearable, all the games were played at night, so we had more than enough spare time to get into mischief. When you have sixteen rascally, unruly teenage boys without adult supervision on one floor of a hotel, you have a recipe for calamity.

Two of the brainier members of our group, roommates Bobby Morris and Paul Schulte, came up with an ingenious way to sleep cooler. The two roommates took the sheets off their beds and tied them together. Then they attached the sheets to the swamp cooler outlet, forming a sail, which directed all the cool air into their room. The invention worked; their room was super cool. Unfortunately, everyone else's rooms got even hotter.

The few adult guests in the hotel were not amused and reported the incident to the front desk. Because we alienated the other hotel guests with teenage inventiveness, we were asked to leave the hotel.

It didn't make sense to me. We were booted out of this dump of a hotel because we invented a way to sleep cool in a sweatbox room. As a seventeen-year-old "C" student, I failed to understand the logic of the manager of the hotel, but nevertheless we moved our belongings across the street to the only other hotel in town, which at the time wasn't much better. With eighteen of us moving out of the dumpy hotel, it was nearly empty. Good business move!

The other hotel we moved into is now the beautifully remodeled La Posada Hotel, the gem of Winslow. In 1994, the Santa Fe Railroad abandoned La Posada Hotel, and plans to demolish it were announced by railroad executives. However, after an outcry from the purists of the Historical Architecture Buildings Preservation group, La Posada was saved by the local residents. It is now the most beautiful hotel in Northern Arizona catering to diehard Route 66 aficionados, but it sure wasn't when I stayed there as a kid.

Benny Lefebvre was not at all pleased with our antics and threatened to make us sleep in the town park if we didn't behave ourselves. So our out-of-control fun days were over for now. We had taken some swings at the system and struck out, but we still had more at bats left during our summer of baseball. However, instead of tempting fate by allowing us to hang out in the hotel all day, Benny planned daily activity trips for the team to keep us occupied, out of the hotel, and out of trouble.

On a day off, we were bussed an hour north of Winslow to the Little Colorado River, where we were taken down the river on speed boats to an idyllic swimming area. It had the serenity and unspoiled rural charm of an oasis in the desert. There were high rocky cliffs that we dove off of into the clear cool water on a sweltering day in Arizona. The day spent swimming in the Little Colorado River and lying in the hot Arizona sun with my teammates was one of the best days of my life. The bonding and camaraderie were things I will always carry with me. This was paradise: playing baseball and living the good life with plenty of money in our pockets.

After three hours of enjoying a picture perfect setting, swimming in the refreshing river, and eating the tasty lunches we had brought with us, we traveled north to the Hopi Indian Reservation where we shopped at the trading post for a couple of hours. There we met and talked with Chief Joe Sekakuku, a Hopi Snake Chief, who signed postcards with his picture on them. This was a special treat for us Californians because we had never seen an Indian chief except in John Wayne movies, and they were actors.

While shopping for "stuff" to bring home, George asked "Chief Joe" to sign a post card with his picture on it. "What's your name son?" Chief Joe probed.

"George Anderson!" He replied.

Frank, Carl, and Billy on a swimming trip to the Little Colorado River in Arizona

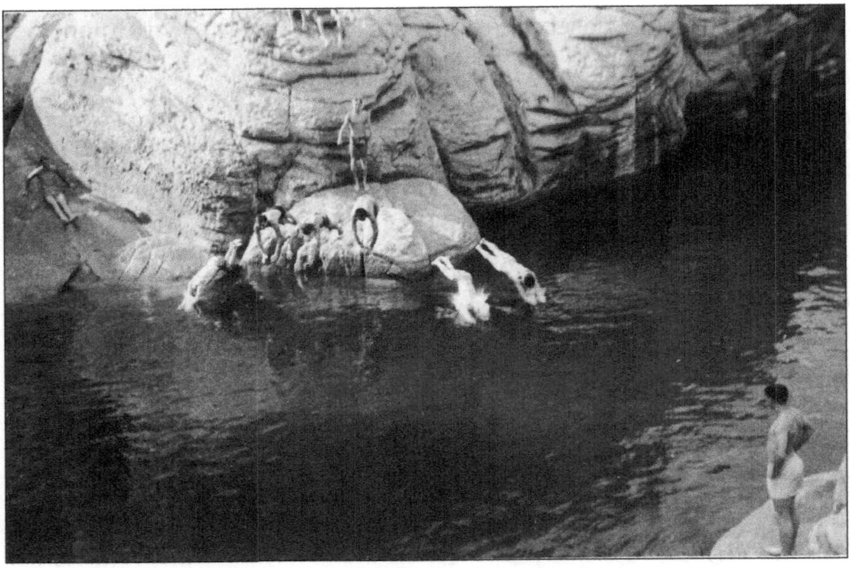

Team diving into the Little Colorado River

George, Mel, and Billy at the river

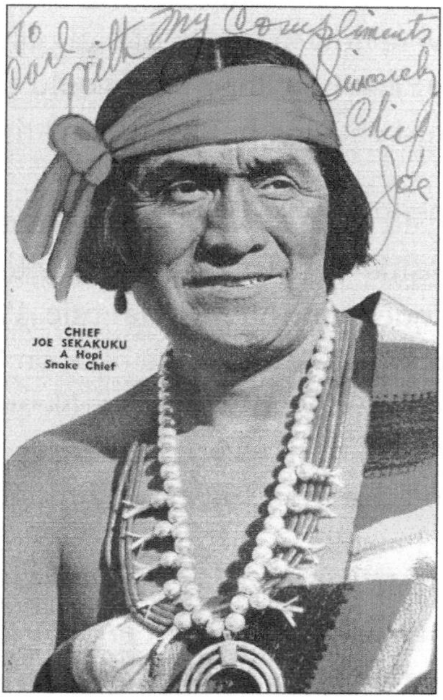

Chief Joe, a Hopi snake chief

Chief Joe stared right through George for a while then spoke very seriously, "That name one day will be famous, but people will not know you by your given name, George." He continued, "You will make lots of money but it won't mean anything to you. Your fame will last forever."

"Thank you, chief, you're very kind." George walked away smiling to himself thinking, "What was that all about? Wow! That chief was really spooky!"

Our stopover visit done in Hopi Land, we loaded back onto the bus headed toward Winslow.

As our bus pulled away, the Chief watched us disappear into the dusty desert with interested curiosity.

• • • • • • • • • •

ON RETURNING TO OUR HOTEL, Benny reminded us that we had been removed from the only other hotel in town and not to repeat the scenario that had gotten us removed. His words weren't necessary because we were now a bunch of ball-playing angels. Yeah, right! He'd find out just how long that would last! We were now conscious of our misbehavior, but we weren't through raising hell by any means.

Having survived Winslow, Arizona—hotel etiquette and breakfast choices aside—we were now ready to venture onto the second leg of our quest for the national title. We had devastated the competition in Winslow and were back on the train, heading for the sectional tournament in Hastings, Nebraska, where more teams were waiting to knock us off our perch.

While asleep on the train traveling through eastern Arizona toward Nebraska, I awoke in the middle of a weird, lucid dream that had Billy Consolo sitting on a red rock mesa. It was flashing by me right out my window. Still in an altered state of sleep, I stared out the window with the scenery rolling by like a movie scene. I spotted Billy on top of a red rock wearing blue tights and a red cape. He was waving for me to get off the train and join him. In my foggy dream state, even as a seventeen year old, I knew something was wrong. It was so surreal! I rubbed my eyes and took a second look, only to observe no one on the rock that was speeding past me. I took a deep breath, smiled, leaned back in my seat, and went back to sleep. Was it that chili I had eaten for lunch?

• • • • • • • • •

WHILE I WAS TAKING A bathroom break away from the other men on the day we mourned Billy, I flashed back to that bizarre apparition I saw on the train traveling through Arizona as a teenager and thought, "Was I hallucinating or was that a precognitive dream that had something to do with Billy and the red rocks? Would he make his presence felt now that we were surrounded by red rocks?" The day was young, but maybe some paranormal incident would occur to confirm my suspicion.

Back in the circle on Secret Mesa, the Arizona sun was becoming warmer as the morning evolved into early midday. Even though it was a perfect fall day and Sedona was at 4,500 feet in elevation, it could get warm in the northern desert. Beads of sweat could be seen on most the seventy-plus-year-old faces. Some removed pieces of clothing and sat on them as cushions on the hard sandstone.

The old timers were starting to feel comfortable with the circle and opening their hearts for all to see their wounded souls. It was a day for letting go of all the heartache and pent up bravado. Also, we were here to establish a clearer understanding of Billy's death and our own mortality, which seemed to haunt us, lurking just around the corner. Billy had died so quickly. Which one of us would be next? Were we here to attain deliverance or to clear the obstacles to understanding of life and death? Maybe by the end of the day we would have some answers? Maybe, maybe not.

Mel Goldberg, who played the important utility position on the team, was now standing and ready to pour his heart out. He looked around at the old men he had known most of his life, but he still didn't feel truly relaxed addressing them. But he pushed himself to address this friendly group of peers.

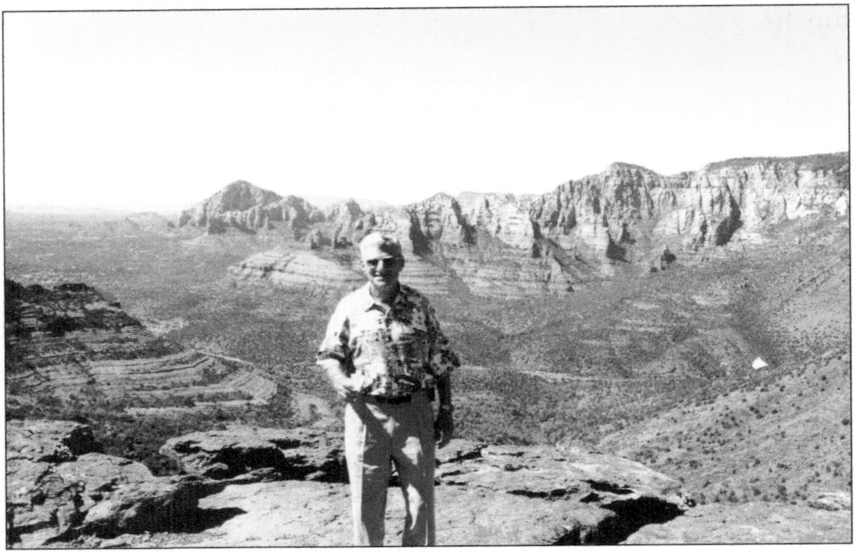

Mel Goldberg

"Billy was my idol. He was everything I ever wanted to be. He was the best high school athlete I have ever seen. He was good looking, funny, smart, and, most of all, he treated everyone he met with total respect."

His bearded face showed heartfelt sorrow and emotional pain. Mel was known for his common sense, intelligence, and great dry sense of humor. He, like the rest of us, had known Billy since childhood and envied him for all the earthly gifts he'd received, but we knew we weren't as lucky as Billy.

"I remember in high school everyone looked up to Billy as a leader and everyone wanted to be his friend. Even though he had a special group of friends that he was close to, he always treated everyone like they were his best friend. With Billy gone, I feel like I've lost a big part of myself. Just being around him made me stand taller and feel better about myself."

Mel looked around to survey his teammates' reactions to his comments. He was a bright and confident man, but he felt vulnerable as his emotions started to unravel. So he cut his speech short by saying, "I loved the man. What else can I say?"

The tall, lanky, white-headed Paul Schulte was the next to get up and speak to his teammates about Billy. "I felt privileged to meet Billy when I joined the team in 1951. Billy was our leader. George and Frank were also both leaders, but Billy was no doubt our main guy. He could do it all on the field, and he seemed older, stronger, and more mature than most of us. He had already had a lot of success at Dorsey High, and because of that we were ready to listen to whatever he had to say. And, of course, he always did have a lot to say.

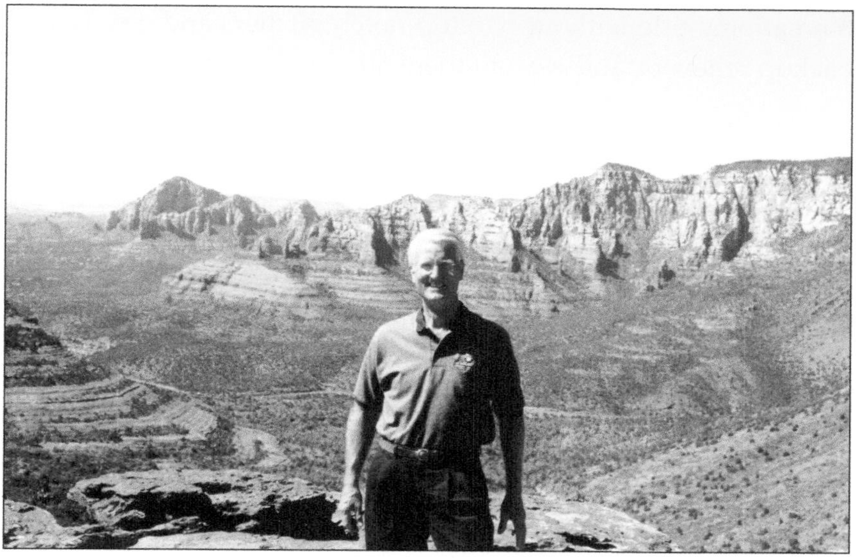

Paul Schulte

"He could back up any talk with his considerable abilities on the field, maybe playing harder than the rest of us, and never causing problems. He was friendly and open, and, even though I was new to the team, he treated me like a long lost brother. I really never got to know Billy like you all knew him until Carl started entertaining us all on our fiftieth reunion in Sedona. Billy's stories were mesmerizing, entertaining, and most of all, very funny."

Paul was an all-league pitcher and the student body president at Loyola High School. Together with Frank Layana, they were probably the best one-two punch pitching duo in American Legion baseball during the summer of 1951. Either of them could make a hitter look feeble when trying to catch up with Frank's fastball or Paul's sharp curve ball. Back then Paul Schulte lived in Glendale, California, and had to commute about fifteen miles daily to join us on the playground at Rancho La Cienaga. He was the only out-of-area player on the team. Paul also proved to be one of the most valuable players on the team. No team could win the national title without two top-notch pitchers and a couple of backup relievers, and we had them all.

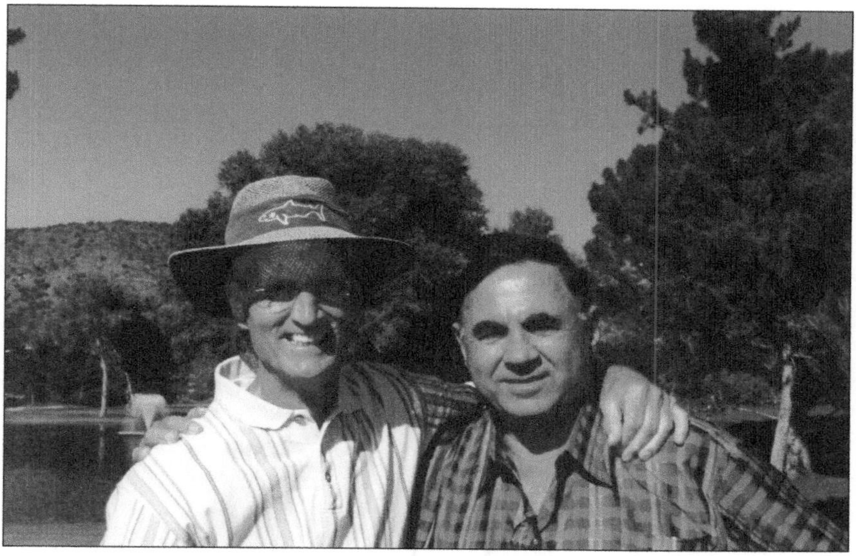

Paul and Frank in Sedona

George being inducted into the Baseball Hall of Fame, standing with Carlton Fisk and Tony Perez

Billy and Frank relaxing and winning in Hastings, Nebraska

13

Fruits, Nuts, and Corn-Fed Farm Boys

THE TRAIN RIDE FROM WINSLOW, Arizona, to Hastings, Nebraska, was about a day and a half long, with stops to switch trains and pick up new passengers. Unlike the overnight trip from Los Angeles to Winslow, this was mainly a daytime sojourn.

When our train pulled into the station, we were greeted by a large contingent of American Legion members. These guys treated us like celebrities and made us feel welcome in an unfamiliar town. They were all World War II veterans, neatly adorned in their Legion uniforms with all their metals, and I was acutely aware that these fine-looking men were the same soldiers who had fought in combat and helped win World War II. Their heroics in Europe and the South Pacific were the turning point in the Allies defeating Nazi Germany and Imperial Japan. Without them, the war most likely would have turned out differently. Now, these veterans were assisting a group of young boys in fulfilling their fantasies as they played baseball all over the country at the American Legion's expense. What an incredible collection of men this was to be sponsoring our idyllic expedition.

By the time we arrived in Hastings, it was twilight. We checked into the hotel with strict instructions from Benny as to our expected conduct. He was not leaving anything to chance. He was on us from the start, and we knew what was expected of us, thanks to lessons learned from our immature behavior at the Winslow hotel. However, our youthful wisdom was still in doubt.

Unlike in Winslow, there were only three teams vying for a chance to compete in the national finals in Detroit and play in Briggs Stadium—later known as Tiger Stadium, home of the Detroit Tigers. The three teams at this particular bump in the road were from Billings, Montana; Omaha, Nebraska; and, of course, our rowdy bunch from Los Angeles, California.

In our first game, we were up against a physically larger team from Omaha, Nebraska, that had flattened all the competition in its state. The Omaha players were typical Midwestern farm boys who were as husky as weight lifters. They had obviously been fed some of that great Omaha beef and had been throwing around bales of hay for years.

On the day of the game, the weather was uncertain with showers appearing off and on most of the day. At night, it was humid and the mosquitoes were attacking us with a vengeance. Being challenged by them was a new experience for us since there had been few mosquitoes in California or Arizona. The mosquitoes distracted us a little bit, but nothing could deter us from our mission at hand.

The Omaha team had touted its infield as the "best in the West." However, that night they did not live up to the slogan. They committed five errors during the game, and we took advantage of every one of them. Frank Layana was the star of this lopsided victory, delivering three hits, including a triple, and driving in three runs. And if that wasn't enough, on the mound he allowed only two hits and no runs in seven innings. Guy McElwaine, the youngest player on our team at fifteen years old, pitched the last two innings and didn't give up any runs, permitting just one hit.

The final score of the game was ten runs for the high-flying trouble makers from Los Angeles, and a big, fat, heifer-sized zero for the Omaha lads. As it turned out, the mosquitoes gave us more problems than the opposing team. After the game, we scratched our mosquito bites until they bled. The Omaha boys were less fortunate than the bugs because their team couldn't even break our skin, much less draw blood.

We had now won six straight on the road, including the doubleheader in Sacramento. So we were playing with high self-confidence, and it didn't look like anyone could stop us. However, Billings, Montana, the next ticket to be punched on our ride to Detroit, was going to try slowing down this out-of-control freight train.

Billings had lost to Omaha the night before, and was now facing elimination if it lost tonight against us, the Los Angeles locomotive. Paul Schulte was pitching for the Golden State boys and was the winner of his previous four games. He possessed a leg-buckling curve ball with great control and a better-than-average fastball.

When Paul took the mound, he knew that he had the best defensive team behind him and an infield that featured four all-league players anchored by Billy Consolo, the All-City third baseman. There wasn't a better fielding shortstop in the country than George "Sparky" Anderson, who could also swing the bat in the clutch. Second base was occupied by the swift Irishman Joe Maguire, who was also of all-league caliber and could run and hit with the best of them.

Paul let the Billings boys hit the ball because he knew his infield would gobble up everything hit on the ground. Anything hit in the air to the outfield would be run down by any of the three fleet outfielders. We could fly and had good arms. Our team had no weakness to be exploited by an opponent. The Billings team hit the ball hard, but the balls somehow always landed in the gloves of the Post 715 players and were registered as outs. Except for a few balls that fell in for hits, it was not a good night for the Billings ball club.

The Billings bunch put up a courageous fight that they could be proud of, but they didn't have enough fire power to match our more experienced group. They were eliminated that night and went home the next day. The score was 6–0 in favor of the ruffians from the land of Hollywood.

In a friendly sportsman-like gesture, the Billings coach, Eddie Bayne, who was a legendary athlete in the state of Montana, donated his team's bats to our dwindling bat supply. Wooden bats, heavier and more breakable than today's aluminum bats, were standard at that time and most of our lighter bats had already been broken by our team. The Billings boys weren't going to Detroit, but at least their bats might be! Even then it was difficult to find a coach with the generosity, kindness, and sportsmanship displayed by the Billings mentor. At the time, we didn't know that Eddie Bayne was a legend in Montana, but his bat donation put him high up in our minds as a man of class and sportsmanship. The pitchers for the Golden Boys had now thrown three straight shutouts while the team was winning seven in a row on the road. Who in the world was going to outshine these terrific athletes from a Los Angeles playground? Could anyone in Nebraska do it?

The last double elimination game and the only one left standing in the way of a trip to Detroit was another night game against Omaha, Nebraska. Omaha wanted revenge for the embarrassing beating it had absorbed two nights prior in the 10–0 loss. They knew they were better than that very bad showing would suggest. So they came out with fire in their eyes and chips on their shoulders. They were not going to be beaten again by a bunch of fruits from California. The Midwest intended to rise and smite the evil Golden State idol.

Marv Nevin, a Nebraska all-state football player and the Omaha all-star catcher, was furious that he had made two costly errors in the first game. He entered the field snorting steam and ready for a battle. He wanted to let us know all about it. He was the biggest athlete among the bunch of big boys from Omaha. He started working on us as soon as the two teams arrived at Duncan Field.

"You stiffs were lucky the other night. You didn't beat us. We gave you the game. You won't get away that easily tonight. We're gonna beat you like a drum all night long and then do it again tomorrow."

He was looking for a verbal fight and didn't care who it was with. He stared at us menacingly, waiting for a brainless sucker to stand up to him. We weren't biting at his oral bait for we had been warned by Benny not to fall into the trap of ego-baiting.

Marv Nevin was trying to distract us from the chore at hand by drawing us into a macho battle of words. He tried challenging our egos, hoping for an opponent with which to tangle! I looked at Billy and George, who, under different circumstances, would have been at his throat by now. They continued to play catch and said nothing, ignoring Mr. Nevin like he wasn't there. Paying no attention to him motivated him to increase the intensity of his verbal baiting. With time running out, he gave it his best last shot.

"You girls from California are all a bunch of pussies! Here, pussy! Here, pussy! There's not a man among you bunch of queers!"

Billy shot a dagger look at Nevin to let him know he had heard him but never moved from his spot on the field. Our lessons in discipline from Benny had paid off, and Nevin's challenging words fell impotent. The fun and games of words were over, and now the real, meaningful contest was about to commence once and for all. Benny's boys had won the pregame wrangle, and now they were ready to play a crucial game.

Marv Nevin was right about one thing; we weren't going to get our way as easily as the first game. This game was a royal battle that lasted over four hours with neither team willing to surrender to the other. The Omaha bunch was extremely somber and wouldn't give an inch to our team for thirteen innings. The highly motivated kids from the beef state gave it their best effort, and although they outplayed the evil empire from the West Coast, they still came up short at 3–2. With the pregame shenanigans and the game lasting four hours, it felt like we were playing all night.

We had won the psychological battle as well as the physical baseball marathon. We had been taught by Benny to show good sportsmanship while on the field. He would remind us, "You play sports for one reason and that is to become skilled at good sportsmanship. If you don't learn proper sportsman-like behavior, then you have wasted your time." That life lesson stayed with us our whole lives.

We were on an eight-game winning streak and headed for Detroit, Michigan, and the American Legion World Series. Out of the 16,300 American Legion teams that started playing baseball in June, there were now only four left, and *we* were one of them.

• • • • • • • • • •

IT WAS SEPTEMBER 2, AND we were back onboard the train to Detroit, where on September 4 we would encounter the first of our three opponents. The game was to be played in Briggs Stadium, home of the Detroit Tigers Major League franchise. For us, walking into that stadium was like walking into the Sistine Chapel because we had never seen a Major League game, much less played in a stadium like this one. There was no Major League Baseball being played on the West Coast or anyplace west of St. Louis until the Dodgers slipped out of Brooklyn, New York, and landed in Los Angeles in 1963. Major League Baseball was something we read about in the sports section of the newspaper but had not yet witnessed.

Beside our Los Angeles squad, there were three other Legion post teams that we would do battle with before we could return home with the world championship—Jacksonville, Florida; Cincinnati, Ohio; and White Plains, New York. These teams were the best of the best and would test us to the max. These three remaining squads would be our toughest competition since leaving California. In particular, Cincinnati and, of course, New York would be as good as, if not better than, the teams we had vanquished in California. But we were up to the challenge and armed with the knowledge that teams from California had won the American Legion World Series the last two years in a row.

The papers in Detroit put us in the driver's seat with headlines that screamed, "LA Boosts Stock for Legion Crown," "LA Team Favored for National Title," and "Farm System Helps Coast Legion Team." The last headline referred to the playground we all played on as "Benny's Farm System," which was a different angle to explain our success growing up together. After those headlines hit the streets, we had large bull's-eyes painted squarely on our backs. Every other team would be out to take aim at the favored team from California, a state that was making a habit of winning the national title. We didn't want to be labeled as the favorites because we understood the additional pressure that would generate for us. But the tabloids had anointed us as the team to beat even before the first pitch was thrown! This put us in the cross hairs of the other three teams' sights and made our goal a greater challenge. Our competition respected us, but they glared at us in a way that made it clear that they didn't like us one bit. We were enemy number one in the city of Detroit! The newspaper articles had set us up for a big tumble with their glowing details about our "superior athletes." Would we succumb to the temptation of believing the hype and become overconfident?

• • • • • • • • • •

BACK IN SEDONA, I HAD brought a newspaper clipping from the Los Angeles Times with me in a folder. It was a nearly half-page obituary on the death of Billy Consolo printed on March 29, 2008. I pulled it out and started reading it for about the tenth time. The headlines spanned the width of the page and in bold black print proclaimed, "Dorsey Baseball Player Went to the Majors at 18."

It told the story of Billy's illustrious days as a super high school athlete who, upon graduation, signed a bonus contract to play for the Boston Red Sox worth sixty-five thousand dollars. In reality, Billy was not ready to go to the majors at eighteen years old. He was a great athlete, but the only reason he went straight to the big leagues at eighteen was a stupid Major League rule stipulating that if a high school player signed for more than four thousand dollars, he had to spend two years with the big club. As impressive as the contract might sound, it prevented him from honing his skills in the minor leagues. Instead he stagnated, sitting on the bench for two years. It was like taking a smart eighth grader and throwing him into college. He was out of his element, way over his head.

It would have been a perfect time for him to enhance his already amazing physical gifts in the minor leagues instead of rotting on the bench. His only claim to fame was as Ted Williams' personal pinch runner. When Ted got on base in the late innings, Billy would get in the game as his runner. Billy was fast and Ted's aging legs were spent, so Billy ran for Ted when he was taken out late in games.

Billy never had a chance to reach his potential for stardom because he was not allowed enough time to develop in the minor leagues. He bounced around the majors with six different teams for ten years, relegated to a utility backup role. It was a testament to his exceptional natural ability that he stayed in the Major Leagues for ten years without proper minor league instruction as a young player. Major League Baseball had broken Billy's heart by not giving him the opportunity to show his outstanding true ability. I don't think he ever got over the frustration of knowing that he never had a fair shot. The newspaper article said it all when it ended by quoting Billy as saying, "I'd have given back all the money if I could have played every day." He was truly in it for the love of the game and nothing else.

Dark monsoon clouds were rolling in from the north, getting closer to the red rocks where we, the remaining sunbaked seniors, were sitting and waiting for our chance to praise the departed Consolo. The northern breeze cooled our sunburned faces. There had been a lot said about Billy, but there was much more to come from the hearts of the men who loved him.

Men in their seventies have pent up passions that boil over on any given occasion that moves them in a heartfelt way. As men grow older their emotions lay closer to the surface of their consciousness, allowing their feelings to easily flow out. I vividly remember my father crying while watching the TV show *Lassie.* The older he became, the easier it was for him to show his emotionally sensitive, feminine side. They say you can't avoid becoming your father, and there I was with my misty-eyed bunch of old friends.

I see the same emotional vulnerability in myself and other men my age. It must have to do with the tail end of a person's life pushing aside all inhibitions and permitting one's true feeling to pour out.

The time-ravaged ex-jocks' emotionally charged bodies were hanging by a thread when it came to discussing Billy's unduly shortened life. Through him, we were confronting our own expiration date, wondering when the end would come for us. Billy's death had been so sudden. What could we learn today that would help us cope with the uncertainty of tomorrow?

Since Billy was without any known illness that would cause sudden death and in excellent shape for his age, I relayed a humorous George Carlin quote. Carlin said this just before he died in 2008: "Life's journey is not to arrive at the grave safely in a well preserved body, but rather to skid in sideways, totally used up and worn out, shouting, 'Man what a ride!'"

It was a great ride for Billy. He had a sweet and fruitful life, but from my selfish perspective, it ended way too soon. Why was he picked to go before any of us other old guys? This question remains unanswered, and might not ever be answered!

Warren "Spud" Johnson was another Dorsey High guy who drove up from Prescott, Arizona, to add his piece of the puzzle to complete our portrait of Billy C.

Warren "Spud" Johnson

Spud was another one of those utility players that no competitive baseball team can win without. If your team is devoid of a guy like Spud, you can't win in a long season. He learned a lot of his baseball skills from being a batboy for the Hollywood Stars in the Triple A Pacific Coast League in the 1940s. In fact, he and George "Sparky" Anderson were batboys on the same team at the same time.

Spud looked great in his uniform, perhaps because he had plenty of professional models to emulate during his batboy days. He also could play any position on the team, including catcher, which made him a valuable player to have on your roster. He now lives in Prescott, Arizona, during the summers with his wife, Jane.

Spud started his eulogy in a different direction. "I won't miss Billy one bit! I won't miss him because I won't forget him. He will always be in my heart and memory. How can you forget someone whom you idolized all your life? Billy is not a person that you would just forget. If you knew him as we did and grew up with him, you would never forget him. I won't miss him because I will think of him daily and have the memories of when we played together. No, I won't miss him one iota … not much, not much."

What more could he say that wasn't already said? It was hard to speak toward the end if you wanted to say something that wasn't redundant or insignificant. Spud was cooked for the day.

Jerry Siegert from Dorsey High was the second youngest player on our team at sixteen years of age. He was a sweet fielding, left-handed, swinging first baseman who, although a year younger than most of us, was a terrific athlete with a smooth approach to the game. As with most of us, he lived in the neighborhood and just a few doors down from Bill Consolo's home.

Jerry Siegert

When we couldn't get to the playground, we played in the streets in front of our homes. Jerry, Billy, and other neighborhood kids played every day according to the sport of the season. Baseball and football were the street sports that we all played then. Jerry had a strict dad who, when it was time for dinner, would whistle for him to come home. When Jerry heard that sound, he immediately dropped whatever he had in his hand—bat or ball—and sprinted home. Billy marveled at the discipline, respect, and maybe fear that Jerry had for his father.

Jerry and I were teammates at the University of Southern California in my senior year. He had played two years of junior college baseball and then transferred to USC.

In his senior year, Jerry was an All-American outfielder for the USC Trojans and played some pro ball. Jerry was another one of our quiet teammates who let everyone else do the talking while he learned about the subject. But I knew that Jerry would have something profound to say about Billy.

"I lived across the street from Billy, and we played in the street almost every day. I would admire the athletic ability this guy possessed. As with any sport he attempted to play, he was faster, stronger, and more agile than any other kid in the neighborhood. When Billy ran past you playing football, it was like you were standing still."

Jerry had lost both of his legs from the knees down in a tragic motorcycle accident in his thirties and walked with a limp most of the time. He never let that incident hold him back from anything he wanted to do in his life. He was as active now as he was before the accident. Today he lives in Bishop, California, with his wife, Mona.

"Billy never flaunted his superior athletic abilities. Sometimes he would slow down and let you win at some game. This is good sportsmanship that one never sees in today's sports. He didn't want to break your sprit with winning all the time, which he could have done. I'll never forget the great athlete that led us to the national championship in 1951. Without him, we would have been a mediocre team at best. I can't think of that Legion team without seeing his smiling face at third base. I know that he's playing third base somewhere up there. God bless you, Billy!" Jerry sat down and wiped his eyes.

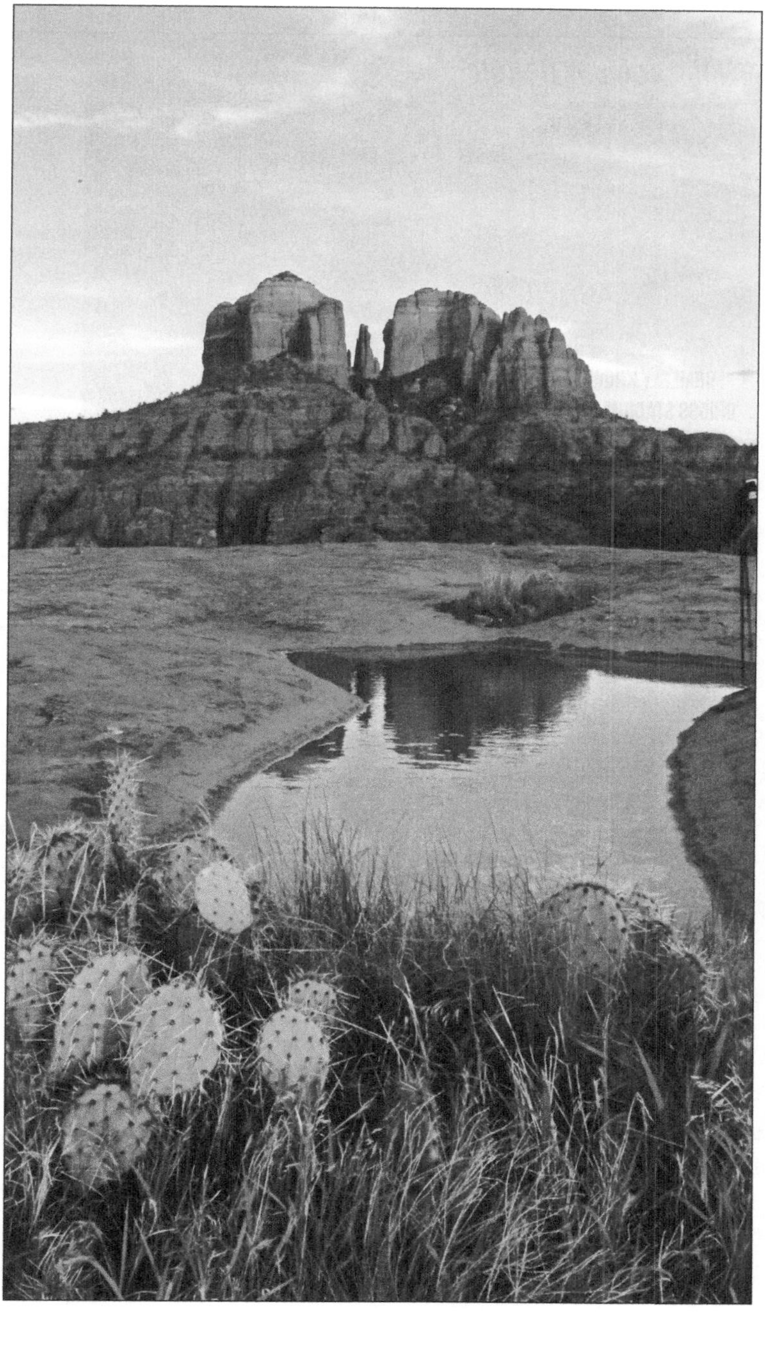

A well-dressed crowd in the 1950s

14
OUR CONSIGLIORE

WE ARRIVED IN THE GREAT city of Detroit on September 2, and, as we checked into our hotel, we were reminded of that eight-letter word that now was etched into our brains—behavior. Our baseball skills were all in order, but this one issue was left to weigh on the mind of Benny Lefebvre. But by this time, we were veteran travelers and the novelty of living in a hotel room had worn off. We had been on the road playing baseball for over a month and were through with kid stuff; we wanted to be men.

Besides, this was the World Series for seventeen-year-olds, and we were deadly serious about not letting this opportunity get away. The odds were that we would never get another chance to play in a World Series again in our lifetime. We did not realize that two of our teammates would eventually participate in "real" World Series games as managers and coaches; George managed a team during three World Series, and Billy coached in one. The rest of us watched them on TV and agonized over every pitch and out.

On September 3, we got a gigantic thrill; we worked out in Briggs Stadium. None of us had ever set foot in a major league stadium, much less played on such a hallowed field. When we ran from the dugout onto the playing field, we were in an altered state that no drug on earth could replicate! The grass was incredibly green and soft, and it was cut just at the right height. It was like running onto a green cloud with bases on it.

As we started to participate in warm-up drills, I felt like I had left my body to watch this ethereal dream from somewhere else. The boys were moving gingerly around like they were dancing on eggs and were very quiet, as if we were playing ball in a sacred cathedral. We were in another dimension that was heaven for all we knew!

Benny broke the silence yelling, "Come on! Get moving! We don't have all day! There are other teams coming later!" George Anderson yelled back, "I'm not leaving; I'm sleeping here tonight." He plopped down on the lush grass and pretended to snore like an ox. Then he started laughing hysterically as we began to throw our gloves at him. Momentarily, we forgot about baseball and returned to a childlike state. This celestial field had magically turned us into ten-year-olds as we frolicked happily around George Anderson. Benny Lefebvre didn't say a word as he watched with a large grin on his face. He just let boys be boys this one last time.

Practicing on a major league field would have been enough for us, but tomorrow we would actually play a game on this holy ground. Our cleats had never touched major league grass. This was a first for the boys from south central Los Angeles.

Then we got another surprising thrill that we were not expecting as Hal Newhowser, the Detroit Tigers' ace pitcher, took the mound to throw us batting practice. He was getting a workout after healing from an injury. We were in seventh heaven—seventeen-year-old kids being pitched batting practice by a major league star after winning eight straight games on the road. And now we were playing for the national championship. Who wouldn't be walking on air?

Newhowser pitched to us at half speed, but we imagined we were playing in the major leagues and hitting against him before fifty thousand screaming fans. We had done this hundreds of times before, but it had been in our backyards playing imaginary baseball by ourselves, narrating every pitch and hit. Imaginary baseball was the main pastime of young ballplayers who didn't have another person to play with. Holding a bat or stick in hand, the player would make up a baseball scenario and then inject himself into the starring role. He was the announcer, batter, and script writer for the make-believe game being broadcast. The game always ended the same way, with the hero clinching the game with a long homerun. It was a lot more fun playing out this fantasy in a major league stadium than in our backyards back home, even though it was all strangely surreal.

The next day we would discover how we would fare against a final four team from Florida. Florida had weather similar to California's, permitting both teams to play baseball year-round.

The teams from Cincinnati and New York were unable to play or practice part of the year because of cold weather and snow. This provided an advantage to the teams from the sunny states. What would happen when two year-round baseball programs tangled? It would be revealed when opening games were played the following day to determine who had the warmest sun: Florida or California.

The inaugural game of the 1951 American Legion World Series was played in Detroit, Michigan, on September 4 between Bentley Post 50 of Cincinnati, Ohio, and Post 135 of White Plains, New York. The two cold weather clubs were to start play at around noon, and later Los Angeles, Crenshaw Post 715, and Jacksonville, Florida, Post 9, would complete the doubleheader.

In the initial game, Cincinnati Post 50 downed the White Plains, New York Post 135 by a score of 6–1. Right hander Howie Whitson of Cincinnati gave up only five hits and allowed no walks to shut down the high-powered offense of New York. Cincinnati had won national titles in 1944 and 1947; by beating a strong team from New York, its players sent out a message to the other three teams that they were going to be contenders this year once again.

Benny had prepared us for this moment by planting that "seed of consciousness" in our minds about going all the way back on the first day of practice. That seed had grown into a small tree, and now we embraced what had been planted months earlier. However, Benny hadn't said, "All the way to the final four." He had said, "*All the way* to the national title."

He reiterated the theme of his first day of practice speech. "Don't be satisfied just to be here in Detroit with the other final three ball clubs. This is not the time to start patting ourselves on our backs and thinking we've arrived, because we haven't."

Benny was short in stature but muscular with handsome features and an infectious smile. He was a master motivator who had coached football, basketball, and baseball with success at all levels.

He had never played professional baseball, but he was a premier student of the game. He seldom made the wrong decision when evaluating an opposing team's player for the right strategic move. He knew us inside out by this point in the season and also knew all the right buttons to push to get us to win.

He continued, "In June, we didn't start out with the intention of ending up second or third. We set our sights on being the best in the world. Out of roughly sixteen thousand teams in the country, we have committed ourselves to being the top dog."

His voice became strained and low, his face unsmiling and somber, but still upbeat. Every eye and mind was focused on Benny, and he knew he had us under his trance.

"This is our last stop to see if we have what it takes to be world champs. Think about that! WORLD CHAMPS!" He shouted louder, "WORLD CHAMPS!"

"Don't let up. Put the pressure on this Jacksonville team, and don't let them get started. Don't look ahead to tomorrow's game.

Let's crush these guys today and worry about tomorrow then. Let's go!"

We all bolted for the locker room door, pushing each other aside to see who could get onto the field first. In our rush to get out of the locker room door, someone stepped on my foot with his metal cleats. It should have hurt like hell, but I was so jacked up with youthful, adrenaline-drenched blood pumping through my veins, I didn't feel a thing. We were ready!

After that we didn't need any additional motivational hype to get us up for the first game in Detroit's beautiful Briggs Stadium. We were consciously locked into our collective goal of "all the way," and this game could take us a step closer. There was no levity in our dugout. This was a serious matter, and we were not taking this game lightly. Everyone had his game face on and his light switches turned on high when the umpire called out the coaches for last-minute instructions.

Moments after the Star Spangled Banner was played, the first pitch was thrown, and we went right to work! Batting first, we scored the first run of the game on Frank Layana's RBI single, and we never looked back.

Frank then took the mound and set Jacksonville down—three up, three down. In the second inning we broke the game open. In my first at bat in a major league stadium I got a key hit, driving in two runs with a long triple to left center. While rounding the bases my hat flew off between second and third base. The radio announcer got more mileage out of my hat flying off than my three-base hit. But I was a happy young man standing on third base puffed up like a blowfish. I had achieved a dream of mine by getting a hit on a Major League field in my first appearance at bat. I felt as light as a feather and was floating in the stratosphere on a natural high. If my life had ended right then, I would have gone to heaven as a happy camper.

Sparky Anderson then doubled me home, and we were flying

high to our ninth straight victory since our last defeat one month earlier in Sacramento, California. We pounded out an 8–4 beating of Jacksonville, although the score did not show the severity of the whipping we handed them. That win against the Jacksonville team elevated our confidence to new heights. We had manhandled a final-four team with not much resistance and had made it look easy.

Our yearly record now stood at thirty-three wins and only three losses. Layana's pitching had stacked up twenty wins against two defeats. Paul Schulte was a winner in twelve games while dropping one. Would Cincinnati give us some strong competition or was it also going to be sacrificed to the golden boys from California? We would find out the next night.

A side note to the game: Briggs Stadium held fifty thousand people, but only eight hundred fans and twenty-six professional baseball scouts attended the game. We didn't care. We had won on a major league field! Besides, it was eight hundred more fans than ever watched us back home at Rancho playground.

With a night game scheduled against Cincinnati, we had some time to spare during the day. A group of us opted to take in a matinee movie at a theater in the heart of downtown Detroit. The movie starred Humphrey Bogart, but, for the life of me, I can't remember the title. We arrived late so we quickly found our seats in the darkened theater. During the movie, we were all making jokes about the lines the actors were speaking and generally being a nuisance to the other patrons. People shushed us to be quiet during the movie. We didn't pay any attention and continued to give our loud commentary on the movie, which wasn't a particularly good one.

When the movie finally ended to our loud applause and yelling, the lights went on in the theater. We looked around and realized we possessed the only white faces in the theater and the other patrons were not at all happy with us. Our row was surrounded by a group of angry young black males who were giving us some commentary about being white and rude at the same time. They were straight from the mean streets of Detroit and had scowls across their faces. They were ready to fight at any sign of resistance on our part. We were frozen in our seats and looking around for the nearest theater exit sign.

At that moment we were not sure if we would be playing baseball that night or, for that matter, any night. It was another example of that eight-letter word getting us in a mess. Once again our behavior had not been favored by others. And this time we didn't have Benny to bail us out. We were on our own and looking for someone to rescue us.

And our aid came from a recognized dependable source, our antidote to conflict and disorder, our Italian consigliore. Billy Consolo stepped forward with a wide smile on his face and his right hand extended, "Hi, my brothers. I'm Bill Consolo, and we're all visiting Detroit from California to play baseball tonight in Briggs Stadium. I'm really sorry for our disturbance during the movie. We were just having a little fun before our game tonight."

Billy, the team's consigliore

One large youth moved aggressively toward Billy, quizzing him, "No shit? You cats are playing baseball tonight in Briggs Stadium? I be living in Detroit all my life, and I ain't never played no fuckin' game in Briggs Stadium."

One of the other black guys interrupted, declaring, "That's 'cus ya'll ain't white, bro." Then he turned to Billy, "You guys get paid any green to play in Briggs field?"

Billy quickly answered, "No, we're amateurs, playing for the American Legion national championship."

The large kid stepped closer to Billy and asked a two-part

question, "How'd ya'll crackers git so far from California, and why does ya'll git to play here in Briggs Field?" This was an era during which integration in baseball was just starting to take place. Jackie Robinson had just been allowed into the big leagues to prove himself, and there was heavy tension surrounding the whole topic of race and baseball. Most of the time, white kids like us were able to ignore the issue, but now it was right in our face.

Billy answered the question in a five-minute, glib dissertation on winning in California, Arizona, Nebraska, and traveling through eight states to finally end up in Detroit and Briggs Stadium. Billy's impressive discourse brought delight and laughter from our adversaries, who were both amused and awed by our accomplishments. Most of them said they had never been out of the city of Detroit, so our feat was beyond their comprehension. Billy's charm had won their respect and our well-being.

Within seconds the hostile barrier between us was eased and friendship ensued. We began to relax in our seats and were exhaling long breaths of stale air, signaling that any peril was behind us.

Before we realized it, the "mean" boys were smiling, standing among us asking questions about baseball and living in California. Sports have a way of bringing people together regardless of skin color, and that was a good thing for us since we were scheduled to play an important baseball game that night.

By the time we left the theater, our new acquaintances were laughing and joking with us and shaking our hands. One guy who had introduced himself as Moe said with brilliant white teeth showing through his smile, "You brothers kick some Cincinnati ass ta'night and we'll be rooting for ya'll." Some said they would attend the game, but none showed up that night. We were happy to get out of there with a group of new friends and all of our teeth. Billy had worked his magic again, and we had dodged yet another bullet, but how many more? Would our luck continue tonight against Cincinnati or were we out of free passes?

Our opponent that night, Cincinnati Post 50, had a number of top quality players who later played in the Major Leagues. Russ and Roy Nixon, twin brothers, were both pro prospects, and Howie Whitson, their ace pitcher, was 26–1 for the Legion summer season. Fortunately for us, Howie had pitched the night before against a tough White Plains, New York, team, beating them 6–1, giving up only five hits while walking none. So thank goodness we would not see Howie on the mound that night.

Paul Schulte, the antidote to good hitting teams, was on the mound for us. Paul had twelve wins with only one defeat. His "out" pitch was his curve ball, which broke sharply and often ended up in the catcher's glove after the hitter had swung over it. Paul pitched very well in important games and this was one of those contests. The state Legion team that won this game would be sitting on easy street, with no losses in the final tournament and perched atop the winner's bracket, waiting for the one-loss team to play for the championship. Both coaches knew this and wanted this game in their win column.

After the national anthem, the game started and nothing happened for eight and a half innings. A fierce pitchers' duel ensued between Los Angeles' Paul Schulte and Cincinnati's lefty, Bill Barnes. I remember watching the game from the bench because a left-handed pitcher was throwing, and I was a left-handed hitter. Benny played the percentages, so when lefties pitched against us, he would play mostly right-handed hitters.

So I was sitting on the bench that night, and it was a nerve wracking game to watch and not play. Each team had opportunities during the game with men in scoring position, but each time the pitchers would choke off the rally. The fate of our stated goal was hanging on the expectation that we could produce at least one run. We were the home team, which meant we hit last in each inning.

The scoreless battle went on for eight and a half innings until we came to bat in the bottom of the ninth inning. Benny was very animated and excited as he yelled, "Okay, who's going to be the hero tonight? What a perfect set-up for a ninth-inning heroic win by one of you guys. Who's going to be the guy?"

Bill Lachemann was the first batter and singled to right field. Don Kenway, next up, asked Benny, "Do you want me to bunt him to second base where he'll be in scoring position?"

Benny thought for a moment, "Naah, you're swinging a hot bat. Hit away!" Kenway stepped to the plate and lashed a long drive that hit the left field fence, 340 feet away. But Lachemann, a slow runner, was the lead person, so it was only a single for Kenway. Mel Goldberg was sent in to run for Lachemann because Benny wanted that winning run on second to be attached to speed. Gordy Sherrett was given the bunt sign and loaded the bases when his perfect sacrifice bunt was booted by the catcher, Russ Nixon.

With the bases loaded, no outs, and our young sixteen-year-old first baseman Jerry Siegert coming to bat, Benny had a tough judgment call to make. Should he send in a pinch hitter for Jerry, who was young and inexperienced, or should he take his chances and let Jerry hit? Benny delayed the game to confer with our business manager, Charlie Wilson, who normally didn't make any on-field decisions. Then Benny put his arm around Jerry, telling him, "Take two strikes before you swing, crowd the plate, and try to work him for a walk."

Benny's strategy was to put the pressure on the pitcher to walk in the winning run from third base. Jerry would be the hero without having to swing his bat. But having Jerry take two strikes before he could swing his bat put an extreme burden on the young first baseman. It was difficult enough hitting in this situation without lugging the extra weight of two strikes on his shoulders. This was the toughest baseball situation Jerry had ever faced in his life as he was fresh off the streets and playgrounds of Los Angeles. It showed on his face. Jerry crept up to the plate with his mind on red alert as a million possible scenarios rushed through his head.

The pitcher delivered a first pitch strike. Jerry winced and fidgeted in the batter's box. The second pitch was also a strike, and now Jerry was in a deep batting hole that most batters dread. He must swing at anything that looked even close to being a strike. He knew that taking a third strike with the bases loaded was a mortal sin in baseball.

He stepped out of the batter's box to take a deep breath and thought, "Another fine mess Benny has gotten me into!"

Jerry dug in and concentrated on the most important at bat of his young life. Bill Barnes, the pitcher, was thinking that Jerry was up there taking the pitch all the way and didn't intend to waste a pitch on him. However, Barnes' next three pitches were out of the strike zone. Jerry Siegert had a good batting eye and had extended his at bat to a full count. With the count at three balls and two strikes, no outs, and the game on the line, Barnes' next pitch was another strike, but this time Jerry swung and connected squarely with the ball. It was a line drive base hit past the first baseman and the ballgame was over.

We had dodged yet another bullet that day, and this one was huge. The whole team, which had been sitting on the bench, charged the field to swarm the hero of the day, Jerry Siegert. Four years later he was an All-American outfielder for the University of Southern California Trojans.

I've known Jerry for fifty-six years, and I don't think that he ever had a bigger hit than he did that night against Cincinnati. Paul Schulte was mindboggling, pitching nine innings of shutout baseball against an excellent hitting team. His curve ball was working to perfection that night, and he pitched most of the night keeping it on the outer half of the plate to a team of good pull-hitters. Paul pitched another shutout for the team. He and Frank had achieved an amazing four shutouts in the last eight games.

We were on a ten-game winning streak, and our overall record was thirty-four wins and three losses. And, most importantly, we were only one victory away from achieving the goal we had set on the first day of practice back in early June.

Earlier in the day, White Plains, New York, eliminated Jacksonville, Florida, 6–0 in the other quarter final contest. Jack Yvars of White Plains rang up his fifth victory of the season, allowing only six hits and one walk and striking out six batters.

Now there were three survivors left to battle each other for the American Legion championship—White Plains, Cincinnati, and the only team without a loss in the final tournament, our Los Angeles frontrunners. The three coaches of each team agreed on only one point—each was positive that his team would win the tournament. The White Plains coach, Mort Grossman, oozed confidence saying, "We lost the first game in the regionals and didn't lose another, not even to the team that beat us the first game. How can we lose?"

Equally confident was Cincinnati's coach, Joe Hawk, who predicted, "Sure we lost 1–0 to Los Angeles yesterday, but we didn't come here to lose. We've won this tournament twice before, and we can win it again."

Benny Lefebvre, coaching the only unbeaten team in the final three—Los Angeles—wore a big smile as he boasted, "We're in the driver's seat, no matter who we play Friday—Cincinnati or White Plains. They've both lost a game. The only way we can lose is to drop two straight. I don't think we will."

The coaches had spoken, and now it was up to the teams to prove their coaches right with wins on the field. Talking about winning and proving it on the playing field against the last teams standing in the country were altogether different tasks. The next night, White Plains and Cincinnati would fight it out in a semi-final elimination game to see who would play us for the national title.

The day of that night game, Benny took us to our first Major

League game, played at Briggs Stadium between the Detroit Tigers and the Washington Senators. To our good fortune, the pitcher that day for Washington happened to be Satchel Paige, the legendary star from the Negro Leagues. Thanks to new integration policies in Major League Baseball, Satchel had finally been allowed to play in "the show." Sadly, his debut in the majors came twenty years later than it should have, and he was now in his middle forties. The West Coast had no Negro Leagues, so we were not familiar with him but Benny filled us in on his super-star status.

His pitching style was poetry in motion. He would wind his throwing arm back in a perfect clockwise circle, bring the ball to his chest, and wait for what seemed to be an eternity, as if to psyche the batter out. "When is that ball coming?" the batter must have thought to himself. Then "Satch" would kick his long, thin leg out high to the front to distract the batter and then shoot the ball like a bullet from his right hand. George would say of Satchel, "This guy's the best pitcher I've ever seen. What a shame he had to wait so long to get to the big leagues."

Of course, we had never seen a major league pitcher before, so we had no talent reference with which to equate Satchel. But we knew he was damn good.

We watched with awe as Satchel Paige pitched his way into our hearts. It was obvious to us that Satch was a superior athlete who should have been pitching in the big leagues his whole career but couldn't simply because he was black. What a shame for the white faces of baseball. He showed them all by being elected to the Hall of Fame some years later.

After letting Satchel Paige entertain us, we went to dinner in the vicinity of Briggs Stadium and later watched the two Legion teams battle it out to see who we would be playing the next night. White Plains, a team that seemed to get better as the season progressed, defeated Cincinnati that night and won the right to play us. Now only one team stood between us and our goal to become national champs. We were thrilled to be in the driver's seat. However, we also were a tad bit overconfident because we knew that White Plains already had one loss. This "one loss thing" caused us to let our guard down, leaving us vulnerable.

This game meant the two big coastal states, one on the east coast and one on the west coast, would fight it out for the national championship. The only difference between us was that we only had to win one game out of a possible two game series. White Plains had to win both. It couldn't have been any better for us. We had lost only three games all year, so losing two in a row seemed out of the question. Besides, we had the almost unbeatable Frank Layana (20–2) on the mound, who was pitching flawlessly since his last loss to Sacramento a month earlier.

We were sitting on top of the world, and it proved to be more than we could handle given our youthful naiveté. Sometimes being too good gets in the way of achieving your goals—or, at least, thinking you're too good. That's what happened to us. We thought that we couldn't be beaten by anyone. We hadn't had a loss in a month, and we were fatigued warriors whose habit of expecting wins had clouded our judgment of how competent our competition was at that critical time. We were just a little overconfident. We had read our press clippings and believed every word.

We took the field against White Plains with great swagger and arrogance and then proceeded to forget to turn on our light switches. We were unconsciously playing baseball without intention. We looked at White Plains not as competition, but as an annoyance on our way to the national championship. Everything we tried that night didn't work. Everything that had worked for the last ten-game winning streak had lost its magic.

For starters, we made three serious errors that cost Layana a game in which he didn't give up any earned runs. His own errant throw on a pick-off attempt led to one New York run, and errors by Joe Maguire and George Anderson brought in two more unearned runs. Even a squeeze play we attempted went as sour as juice from a lemon.

With Layana on third base and one out, the batter missed the squeeze play sign, and Frank, who was running on the play, was tagged out at home plate. It was bad baseball with mental errors, missed signals, physical errors, and no hitting in the clutch. All the solid playmaking and sacrifices we had performed to perfection for a solid month went south on a night we thought we were going to be national champs. We asked ourselves, "What happened to all the winning lessons we had learned throughout the summer?"

Benny had an answer to that question: "Nothing works when you play lousy baseball and you forget about turning on your light switch all night. Executing plays properly is the name of the game, but you forgot about the importance of the game you were playing."

Benny was visibly upset with our uncharacteristically ragged brand of baseball, which he took personally as our coach. It was not the way he had trained us to play the game. As we were getting on the bus to return to our hotel, he yelled at us like a strict father scolding his naughty children.

"You guys decided to turn off your light switch and go to sleep on the night we could have been world champs. What a bunch of bozos!"

We lost that nightmarish game 3–1 when we should have won 2–0. Frank allowed seven hits and no earned runs but lost his third game in twenty-three starts. The only games he lost all season had been games in which he was either wild or we blew the game with errors. With a little support and better control, he could have been 23–0 for the season. Oh, well. As they say, you can't win them all! We just thought we *should* win them all!

We still had one more game to play and one more game to win before our destiny would be complete. That loss to White Plains, New York, sent us a very loud wakeup call the next morning. We didn't have much time to dwell on the defeat as we were scheduled to play the national championship final game at 11:00 AM.

Benny Lefebvre wasn't about to let anyone forget the goal that we all had pledged to achieve back on June 1. We knew what we had to do to fulfill our season, our summer, and our lives. He spoke to us one last time as our coach, starting with one of his esoteric statements: "Gentlemen, good judgment comes from experience, and useful experience comes from bad judgment." I thought, "What is he talking about?"

Then he took us down a more conventional road of thinking, which better suited our intellects. "In other words, we learn from our mistakes, plain and simple. You guys have come too far to let this opportunity get away. You've poured out your sweat and guts to get to this point. Now you must finish it. Turn on your light switch!"

Benny's half-bald head sported an oily, sweaty film that I had not seen before. The stress of this last game was showing on his usually controlled facial expressions. He mopped his shining head with a towel and then wiped his face. His features were exposing the residue of a long and tough summer of coaching. The look on Benny's face cried out, "I'll be glad when this final game is over!" He was drained.

His speech was clear and quiet, but he left no doubt. Every phrase was emotionally charged as Benny was not one to mince words. His forte was being a motivator, but he wasn't prone to being a carnival barker type. His style was similar to a priest preaching to his congregation.

"Play this game with great care and awareness because I promise you that if you don't, you'll play it over and over in your minds for the rest of your lives. This game will become a very pleasurable memory or a nightmare. Either way, you won't be able to get it out of your head. Play with intention and instinct but not fear—the same way you play on the playground in LA. It's in your hands now, so go out and play your best."

We were not afraid of anyone. We knew we would have won the night before if we had played up to our usual standards. Now we had no choice but to bounce back with the best game of our young lives.

"This is the best team I have ever coached … and I've coached some damn good ones. Don't let yourselves down. We've set our hearts and minds to win this thing. Now let's get out there and get the job done!"

Let the battle begin!

Billy Consolo, a.k.a. Superman

15

Battle to Be the Best

It came down to one last regulation game between White Plains, New York, and Los Angeles, California, to determine who would be the American Legion Baseball World Champions. With two of the biggest states fighting for the coveted prize, it didn't get any better for the American Legion World Series. This was the definitive contest in amateur baseball. The next step up was professional baseball and to play for pay.

After one more year of high school baseball, many of the players on these two teams would turn professional at the young age of eighteen. Three names—Grover Jones of White Plains and Billy Consolo and Frank Layana of Los Angeles—had baseball scouts salivating at their superior talents. When this trio left high school in 1952, they all signed large bonus contracts with major league teams. But this day they would play one of the most important games of their unpaid careers.

Grover Jones, the catcher for New York, was a boy in a man's body. He was more physically developed than any player on either team. He was actually bursting out of his uniform. He was five foot ten and weighed 185 pounds without an ounce of fat on him.

He was built like a lumberjack. Grover was a left-handed batter with remarkable power in his large upper body and bulging, muscular arms. He could hit to all fields with prodigious power. This seventeen-year-old kid was the real deal, and he could do it all. He was a great three-sport, all-American athlete from White Plains High School who signed a professional contract with the Chicago White Sox in 1956. He made his promising debut with the Chicago White Sox on September 8, 1962, but, unfortunately, in 1965 his career was cut short because of a severe shoulder injury. Grover was ready to show his exceptional ability in the game to be played before nearly two thousand loving fans of amateur baseball.

The game started at 11:00 AM on an overcast day in Detroit. We were the home team, so we were on the field first. When we first ran onto the field, we were brimming with confidence. Our red hot pitcher Paul Schulte was on the mound, and he had thrown a shutout two nights before against Cincinnati, an excellent hitting team. We were ready for New York, even if the Yankees had shown up. I was playing right field on that unforgettable day and turned to the bleacher seats behind me. I saw the sign that read "360 feet" on the right centerfield fence. I thought to myself, "No one is going to hit one that far." It would take Mickey Mantle's power to hit it out of this park.

In the first inning, I was proven wrong. With two men on and one out, New York's clean-up hitter, Grover Jones, the muscle-enhanced lefty, found a fastball right in his wheelhouse that met the sweet spot of his bat. The ball took off like a skyrocket headed for the right field bleachers behind me. At the loud crack of the bat, I took off running full speed toward the fence. I looked up and saw the ball streaking well above my head, banging into the empty right field bleacher seats above the 360 foot sign.

My heart stopped beating and tears started forming in my eyes. I was heartbroken with a hollow empty feeling in the pit of my stomach. Was I going to cry in front of all these people?

Certainly not! I had to pull myself together and convince myself that we could still win this game. We were down 3–0, and we hadn't even been up to bat yet. I prayed Paul Schulte wouldn't give up any additional runs in the inning. For our team this was a depressing development because we were not accustomed to trailing in the first inning. How would this event play out in our fragile psyches after losing to this team the night before?

After the inning ended with no further damage, we entered the dugout with our heads hanging in distressed confusion. After only a half-inning, it was obvious we were on the ropes and barely hanging on. Could we hurdle adversity and fight back or would we die a tormented death one win shy of our championship goal? It showed in our body language with stooped shoulders and glassy eyes. At this point the national championship appeared very far away and our summer dream was fading fast.

We had not dodged that bullet. We had taken it right between the eyes, and it might have been fatal, if it were not for Superman. Yes, Superman to the rescue! Well, not the comic book Superman, but someone with the same name. Consolo rushed into the dugout, screaming with fire in his eyes. His Italian temper was aflame. No stooped shoulders and teary eyes for that guy.

"Don't anyone get any ideas about getting down or giving up! We're gonna get those three runs back and more this at bat!" he declared.

He pointed and shook his finger at no one in particular, which was his personal trademark. He continued his lecture: "If anyone hangs their head, I'm gonna kick his ass." And we knew Superman could do it, too. "We're a better team than these guys, and now we're gonna prove it."

Billy had the proverbial "fire in the belly," and it was contagious! We looked into Billy's eyes and we saw the consummate warrior, a ballplayer who would never quit and wouldn't let us quit either. Billy's exceptional physical abilities were only exceeded by his fierce desire to win at any game he was involved in. We got the message loud and clear. The attitude in the dugout completely changed from dejection to confidence. We were a bruised and bloodied boxer who was about to knock out his opponent. You could see the bravado and swagger return; our faces now wore grins and our body language spoke of our determination. This transformation happened in just two minutes, thanks to Billy Consolo.

With that resounding challenge still ringing in our ears, we slapped ourselves, stopped feeling sorry for our plight, and went to work to get those runs back. It would not be easy, but we had a promise and a destiny to fulfill. In our minds, there was no such thing as quitting. We had seen the light!

Our second hitter, Joe Maguire, got a base hit to start our rally. Consolo worked the pitcher for a walk, and then Frank Layana was safe on an error by New York's second baseman. With the bases loaded, Bill Lachemann singled in two runs. With runners on second and third with two outs, Don Kenway got a clutch single to drive in two more runs.

Thanks to Superman, who wouldn't allow us to quit, we had scored their "three runs and more" for a total of four to their three. We were now leading 4–3, thanks to the clutch hitting of Bill Lachemann and Don Kenway.

In the top of the second inning, Paul Schulte settled down and his curve ball started breaking sharply. New York hung a zero on the scoreboard for the inning. The bottom of the second inning again was ours to extend our lead. With timely hitting, including a booming triple by Paul Schulte and the third RBI hit of the game for Bill Lachemann, we scored three more runs in the second inning.

The score after two innings was Los Angeles 7, New York 3. It only got worse for New York as we added three more runs in the next three innings on two more hits and two more RBIs for Don Kenway, to go up 10–3. Don Kenway was on a tear. Every ball he hit was a laser shot—totaling three hits and four RBIs—and we were only in the fifth inning. Don had come to the park prepared to contribute his red hot bat to the cause of a national championship. It was the success story of our team; someone always picked us up when we needed it. Throughout the entire season each of us was a contributing factor at some time or another.

Superman had awakened the sleeping giant from the Golden State. New York came back in the top of the sixth inning with three runs, looking like they might make a run at us. They had a very skilled hitting team, and, with Grover Jones in the lineup, no lead was safe. Paul Schulte was in trouble in both of the next two innings, but, with a great play at shortstop by George Anderson and a well-placed strikeout, he worked through it.

New York would not give up without a fight, but in the long run they just ran short of outs. A team only gets twenty-seven outs in a regulation game, and the New York team had just spent their last one. The game was ours to savor. White Plains, New York, had come back, but it was too little too late. We won the biggest game of our lives 11–7 and with it the American Legion World Championship. It was my thrill of a lifetime!

From right field I threw my hat up in the air and yelled, "We did it! We did it! We're the best in the world!"

I sprinted to the pitcher's mound to join my teammates who were forming a large dog pile on top of pitcher Paul Schulte. We yelled and screamed and carried on like a band of invading Huns who were pillaging a village. We rolled around on the major league grass until our uniforms were covered with grass stains and wet from our sweat. We were reveling in the greatest baseball win any of us had ever experienced in our lives. The excitement seemed to turn my stomach upside down. For a minute, I thought I might throw up or have diarrhea right there on the field. I felt like I was outside of my own body, like I was watching the celebration from somewhere else.

We had come to the end of our summer-long odyssey and, as world champions, we believed in our hearts that we had earned it. Benny came up to each player, thanked him, and gave him a big hug to show his gratitude for what each of us had done for the team championship. We also thanked him for teaching us how to play the game of baseball his way. Benny Lefebvre was the main reason we were national champs. Yes, we had terrific athletes, but without his leadership and unyielding new way of thinking, we would still have been stuck playing one dimensional baseball. And one-dimensional teams don't win world championships.

Benny dragged us kicking and screaming into the wonderful realm of Benny Ball, which wasn't anything like the way we thought baseball should be played. We faced close scores and extra innings in many must-win games, but always triumphed in the end. These victories were manufactured by Benny's Zen-like strategies and game plans.

He would not let us quit when we were down, which taught us how to be winners. When Benny picked us off the playground, we were superior but selfish and self-centered athletes. He stripped us of our me-oriented egos obsessed with compiling gaudy statistics and shaped us into a bunch of hard-nosed, selfless ballplayers who played to win together as a team.

Without Benny, we still would have had a lot of fun playing baseball together, but we never would have played outside of California. He taught us to stick together when the going got tough and rely on each other. No doubt about it, Benny showed us how to win and not just by telling us how to win; he took us by the hand and led us to victory. As he would say, "Trust your teammates to do their job, and they will trust you to do yours. Fail to honor your teammates, and they will fail to honor you. No one person on a team can be a winner alone."

Our national championship was a team championship. Everyone on the team was responsible at one time or another for our success. Benny showed us by his example how to be winners on the field and off. We carried and practiced his teachings throughout our lives.

Although the batting honors for our team went to Don Kenway, Bill Lachemann, and Paul Schulte, the real unsung hero was Superman with his wake-up call that awoke us from our slumber. But make no mistake about it, without Don Kenway and Bill Lachemann's timely hitting, we would have been runners-up to New York. The two of them drove in seven of our team's eleven runs.

The kid with the big biceps, Grover Jones, won the Most Valuable Player award for the tournament after hitting that impressive three-run homer in the first inning. He finished the day with two hits and five RBIs. He was later named the 1951 National American Legion Player of the Year. Grover had narrowly beaten out Billy Consolo for that award; both deserved the recognition.

But that day, even with all his impressive stats, he couldn't out duel our Superman, who had no hits in the game but delivered the most important motivational speech of his young life. With his impressive ability to sway people's thinking to his side, he could have been a lawyer.

We had fulfilled our destiny and made good on our promise to bring home the championship to Rancho La Cienega Playground in Los Angeles. Out of 16,299 other teams in the country, we were the last one standing. The city of Los Angeles had not won an American Legion National Championship since Sunrise Post did it in 1942, and they have not won another one to this day.

We celebrated our victory, this time without feeling the need to trash the hotel. That was kid stuff. We had started this journey as raw, immature juveniles and had transformed into men in just a month or so. Being a man, we found out, is a matter of how you feel about yourself inside and has nothing to do with age. We felt like men, therefore, we became men.

We gathered in Billy and George's room and ordered up food and sodas. Joe Maguire and Mel Goldberg were smoking cigarettes while the rest of us, who didn't normally smoke, had purchased cigars and were puffing away. There was so much

"AMERICAN LEGION JUNIOR BASEBALL PLAYER OF THE YEAR"

GROVER JONES, Jr., White Plains, N. Y., catcher and team captain was the unanimous choice of the Hall of Fame Committee at the National Finals, in Detroit, for the selection as the 1951 "American Legion Junior Baseball Player of the Year". Jones' picture will be placed in The American Legion plaque in the National Baseball Hall of Fame and Museum at Cooperstown, N. Y.

Jones also won the National Batting Championship with an average of .408 for all National Tournament games.

smoke billowing everywhere you could hardly see anyone across the room.

Billy raised his bottle of Coke and yelled, "To all us pussies from the great city of Los Angeles who are now world champs! I say screw all those people who said we couldn't do it!" Then he added, "We're the best in the world! End of story!"

Amidst roaring laughter we hoisted our soda bottles and drank to the toast of the night. There was so much deafening noise in the small room you couldn't hear anything. Some of the guys were replaying the game over and over with piercing exuberance. Billy could barely get a joke off the ground.

"This guy wearing a world championship jacket and a beautiful blond on each arm walks into a bar." The small room erupted into earsplitting boisterousness, and he never got another word out of his mouth all night. It was just one of those nights!

We were finally living our long-shot dream of being the best in the world. No one could ever take that away from us. As we partied into the night the parade of fun was barely getting started. We were anxiously anticipating our return to Los Angeles and all our families, friends, and schoolmates. We had a long, two-day trip back home and didn't have a clue about what would be waiting for us at the train station when we docked in Los Angeles.

• • • • • • • • • •

THE TWO-DAY, TWO-NIGHT TRIP FROM Detroit to Los Angeles felt like a week because we were so anxious to get back home to our families and friends. School had started in California around September 1, so we had already missed a week or so. But no one cared because we were now the world champs. Our train pulled into Los Angeles's Union Station at about 10:40 AM on Tuesday, September 11, 1951.

The first ballplayer off the train was Billy Consolo, who was carrying the large trophy that signified we had indeed won the national championship. He was all smiles and ready to meet his fans, family, and girlfriend. He was the star, and he knew it. He was going to shine brightly for this big crowd. His already big smile widened in preparation for the adulation he was about to receive from his loving fans and friends.

The first people we met getting off the train were the welcoming committee of the American Legion Post 715—our sponsors. They were dressed in their Sunday uniforms, which were usually reserved for special occasions. We hugged them and thanked them for their support, and then we were quickly whisked away to encounter the waiting boisterous crowd.

The paper said that there were five hundred people there to greet us, but it sounded like five thousand shrill, radical rebels. The schools had sent their bands and cheerleaders there to add to the chaos. It felt surreal after having just completed a relatively quiet two-day trip on the train. To walk off the train into a thunderous mass of people was unnerving to say the least. My mind was still adjusting to the soothing clitter-clatter of the railroad tracks when suddenly I had to deal with the deafening clamor of five hundred people and two bands. There were large banners being held by students welcoming us home. Even our parents had found time to be there to usher us back to reality. It was great seeing them again after a month away from their influence and comfort.

My dad was there dressed to the hilt, wearing his usual hat and big smile. "You did good son! You did real good!" he yelled over the crowd. My mother grabbed me and squeezed hard while tears of joy leaked from her eyes. They were both very happy to have their son back.

Suzy Sorensen and Carol Valle, my two favorite girls from the playground, were among the Dorsey High School students who came to welcome us home. Suzy came over to me and gave me a hug and a peck on the cheek, yelling over the crowd noise, "Great job! You guys are bitchin'!"

I gazed into her blue eyes and thanked her, "Thanks for being there for us all summer and being here today." She then ran off to be with Billy, and I knew precisely where I stood with her. Superman had won over the beautiful damsel once again.

Carol was draped around her future husband, George, and wouldn't let go. After a month apart they were overjoyed to see each other.

Another Dorsey High student, Tom Seeberg, was also there to welcome us back. He was our student sportswriter who supplied the two major newspapers with the scores and stories about our games throughout our long season. He had been with us as we conquered California and after we left the state behind, we also left Tom. It was great seeing him again.

Politicians were there to glad-hand anyone breathing and to be noticed by their constituents. Photographers and reporters were there to get their story of the day about the local Cinderella team that had outshined 16,299 other teams in the country. It was a three-ring circus, and we were the freak show. But we were a very weary bunch, trying to appear like we were enjoying ourselves.

After a while, it became tedious and I felt like a piece of meat in the grocery store, people staring at you as they passed by. My nerves were starting to short circuit because I was not accustomed to the constant cacophony of shouting and loud music. Being a celebrity even for a day didn't feel satisfying to me. I remember at some point wanting to jump into my parents' car and drive home. But that wasn't going to happen because they had the whole day planned out for us.

The bands played on as the welcoming committee did their thing with speeches and trophy presentations. Each of us was introduced to the crowd with a resounding roar of approval. Countless pictures were taken of our victorious baseball team, with Billy Consolo and Frank Layana lighting up most of the flash bulbs. After an hour and a half, the wild welcoming committee dispersed into thin air and we were whisked away in a fleet of convertibles to the private home of Mrs. Janet C. Wilson, the wife of Charlie Wilson, the Legion representative for our team, for a barbecue luncheon with our parents.

The first day of celebration was over, but the city and our sponsors—Marshall and Clampitt DeSoto dealers—were not finished feting their newly crowned celebrities. Numerous testimonial dinners and luncheons were given in our honor in the following weeks. We were given many gifts, and each player had a personal story written about them to be read at the testimonial events. We were star guests at the Ice Follies and two or three minor league baseball games. When would this lucid dream end? Not for some time, as the elite prize was yet to come in October.

Frank, Benny, and Billy

The winning team of the American Legion World Series received as a grand prize an all-expense-paid trip to see two games of the 1951 World Series. Because the two teams playing that year were both from New York City—the Yankees and the Giants—our team would fly from Los Angeles to New York City to attend games three and four of the series at the historic Polo Grounds.

None of us had ever journeyed east of Detroit, which we had only just visited because of American Legion Baseball, so of course we had never explored fabulous New York City. Games three and four of the World Series were being played on the sixth and seventh of October. We had a month to prepare for our dream trip to New York City and to attend our first World Series games. In the meantime, we were still being invited to various functions that wanted to piggyback on our success. During these affairs, we would be introduced to the audience and receive a round of applause. The fickle public soon found other celebrities to chase, and, finally, toward the end of the month our popularity ran its course until we were old news. American Legion champs? Who's that?

The real World Series was approaching and the Dodgers and the Giants were in a dog fight to represent the National League in the Fall Classic. It wasn't settled until October 3 in the last game of the three-game playoffs when Bobby Thomson's three-run homerun in the bottom of the ninth beat the Dodgers, 5–4, for the Giants' right to play in the series. His homerun was called the "shot heard 'round the world." It is still considered to be one of the all-time classic games in baseball history.

With all the external stimulation swirling around us, attending classes was a very difficult task. How could a kid keep his brain on algebra with a trip to New York City and the World Series looming in our near future? School seemed like an afterthought and was totally irrelevant to us for the remainder of the month of September. We existed in some other dimension that had no relationship to schoolwork or studying. We strutted around in our new jackets with a baseball insignia on the front that simply announced "WORLD CHAMPS 1951." We were celebrities at our respective schools; even our teachers were in awe. And in our school the teachers were Jesuit priests who were also in awe of a higher power. Maybe they imagined us to have special favor with God himself—heady stuff for a bunch of seventeen-year-olds.

As September eroded away, we were prepared to meet

October and the World Series head on. We would be flying out of Los Angeles International Airport on Trans World Airlines on our first cross country flight, landing in the Big Apple. Our estimated date of arrival was October 5, 1951.

National champs in Briggs Stadium, 1951

Team posing at Polo Grounds in New York City while holding championship banner

16

A Bite of the Big Apple

I REMEMBER THAT THE LAST WEEK before we flew to New York City was a blur in my consciousness. Between trying to do some schoolwork, getting packed, and receiving instructions from everyone about what to do in Manhattan, my brain was in a fog most of the time. I talked to my teammates, and they were in similar mind freezes, so I didn't feel so bad about being so disoriented. I had taken many pictures during our month on the road—all in black and white—but this time I would be taking the family 16mm color movie camera with me. I was excited about filming movies of the great skyline of New York City and maybe the World Series. Having lived in Los Angeles most of our young lives, we were all fascinated by the mysterious glitter of the most famous city in the world.

We had been told New York City was the ultimate in nightlife and fun, and we wanted to experience it. We were well past the stage of abusing our hotel. We were ready to take on a major metropolitan area. Our maturity had blossomed halfway through the season, and we no longer had time for kids' games. We were men now, men who wanted to taste the sweet magical forbidden secrets of New York City. We had passed our rites of passage on the playing field and now wanted to know what it would be like to be men visiting New York City.

Finally the day we had all been waiting for arrived—the morning of Friday, October 5, 1951. The trip became even more historic as we became the first American Legion national champions to fly to the World Series. In previous years, the winning teams had traveled by train. It was a big deal for us as only the wealthy and famous flew coast to coast at that time. We flew on a DC6 four-engine propeller plane out of Los Angeles International Airport and landed in La Guardia Airport on the other coast. Flying time was only about five or six hours. This was the ultimate in the new space age aircraft equipment America was producing after the war; commercial air travel was in its glamorous infancy.

At this time, it was very prestigious and sexy to fly coast to coast, and the passengers dressed up for the occasion. Women wore furs over their designer dresses with veiled hats and high heels. Men were wrapped in expensive, tailored suits with broad-brimmed hats and brightly shined shoes. Men were not seen without ties and women were bright-eyed with heavy makeup. It was a contest to see who could out-dress the other. Air travel was not for fashion-challenged paupers. It was only for the glitzy rich!

Then we showed up on the tarmac, and we were neither glitzy nor rich. We were decked out in our new championship jackets and corduroy pants. We were full of youthful energy and anxious to get airborne.

An overdressed, snobbish woman with a strong New York accent looked at her husband, "Why are they letting these young punks on our flight? How dare them!"

"We just got the luck of the draw, Mable!" He responded smiling.

"When we get to New York I'm going to complain to the supervisor," she uttered in a whining tone.

Nevertheless, we were getting on board, and the affluent

commuters were about to experience the most memorable flight of their wealthy lives.

The American Legion posts in Southern California were still milking our status as champions. They had set up a photo opportunity for a parting portrait of the team standing on the movable stairs going into the body of the plane. At the bottom of the stairs, two American Legion executives, Commander Tim Benson of Post 188 and a past commander, Bill Kreitz, were shaking hands with our coach, Benny Lefebvre.

The picture would run in all the papers and Trans World Airlines would get its plug, of course. I was taking movies of the guys until the photographers started shooting the team, then I just moved next to Benny, who was busy shaking hands. Before I knew it, someone had stuck a flight bag in my hand with large letters spelling out TWA. I had been duped into becoming part of the propaganda machine.

Congratulations before flying off to New York City and the World Series

This whole process took about half an hour, which held up the boarding of the paying customers, who were not happy about the delay. We were seated first since we were standing on the stairs of the plane. For obvious reasons, the airline did not seat us together. Now why would they think that we would be a potential problem? We were just a bunch of young innocent angels winging our way to New York to watch a couple of World Series games!

The plane took off without incident and the well-dressed passengers snuggled into their seats for the eastern migration of this elegant, featherless iron bird. The first hour of flight was uneventful as the ants hadn't crawled into the players' pants yet. Boredom became apparent in the second hour of flight since sitting still for hours at a time was not our strong suit. The ants came to life as a pillow was thrown toward George Anderson's seat among the paying customers. It was thought to have been thrown from the area where Billy Consolo sat, but no confirmation was forthcoming. Since they had scattered us throughout the plane, it became apparent that throwing pillows was our only way of agitating each other. We could not stop annoying each other for even the six or so hours that it took to get to New York.

The pillow had missed its intended target and hit a fashionably dressed woman, knocking her hat off. She immediately pushed the button above her seat, which summoned the flight attendant. While the attendant asked the irate lady what she wanted, another pillow was on its way to another target wearing a baseball jacket. Every time the attendant would face the area from which the pillow was thrown, another one would be launched behind her.

This resulted in laughter even among the sophisticated clientele. It became apparent that pillow throwing had become the latest fashion trend as a smiling, diminutive, gray-headed lady stood up and threw a pillow at no one in particular. This elderly, elegant woman wore deep lines on her face with unabashed honor. It was obvious that she had lived a full and productive life and was now alone. She was at a point in her life where she was going to take every opportunity to have some fun, and she didn't care what people thought of her actions. When people live long, useful lives, they tend to lose their inhibitions as they get older and, therefore, have more fun than they did when they were young. She had a wispy smile and searching eyes that surveyed everything in one sweep.

At the time, I remember wishing that this wonderfully alive, charming older woman were my grandmother because of how much fun she would be to have around. She relished the fact that the whole plane was watching her. Grandma was in the spotlight, and she was going to shine for her admirers. As she backhanded the pillow with her left hand toward the aisle, she let out a loud belly laugh, raised her left fist, and then promptly sat back down. Her animated image has lived vividly in my mind since that day.

This took place at a time in our country when there was much less tension than today and people had a sense of humor. We didn't have the anxiety of terrorists being on board and uptight attendants who would overreact at the slightest disruption. The aviation industry was an infant, and no one had any idea how perilous it would become sixty years in the future. With all the hoops you have to jump through these days just to get on a plane, flying has ceased to be fun.

This was a case of some fun loving teenage boys having an impromptu pillow fight, which would cause no harm and maybe even delight some of the stiffly dressed, bored passengers. The flight attendant knew she was outnumbered and outwitted and quickly retreated to her station. She wasn't about to report to the captain that there was an inoffensive pillow fight in progress on his aircraft.

Actually, it never evolved into a full-fledged, take-sides pillow fight. Rather, it remained an intermittent shower of soft, fluffy pillows, delivered by even some of the more fun loving travelers. The additional paying flyers just ignored the pillow melee, kept reading their books, or dozed off. As long as things didn't get out of control, people were having fun with it, and the "boys will be boys" premise prevailed as usual! What else could one expect aboard an aircraft loaded with sixteen precocious teenage boys?

At the beginning of the flight, the captain on the intercom had welcomed us on his flight. He mentioned what we had accomplished, so the swanky commuters felt comfortable with us knowing that we were more like eccentric celebrities than volatile delinquents. The rest of the flight was smooth sailing, with only an occasional airborne pillow floating by with maybe a hat or two dislodged from someone's head. Toward the end of the six hour flight, all of the sixteen teen ballplayers were asleep, and I'm sure all of the other passengers were grateful.

The large propeller-driven plane was preparing to land and women replaced their hats, which had been removed by pitched pillows, in preparation for their departure from the aircraft. Upon leaving the plane, many passengers came up to us to send us off on our venture into New York City.

Even the snobbish woman with the heavy New York accent who had labeled us punks at the beginning of the flight came to wish us well.

"Thanks for the laughs, boys! I don't think I've ever enjoyed a flight as much. It was reminiscent of my youthful days. Have fun at the World Series and also visiting the city!" she exclaimed, smiling at us as we descended the stairs to the tarmac, proceeding toward the baggage area. My feeling was that most of the departing passengers felt we had made their flight time pass more amusingly and enjoyably. Being captive on a flight with sixteen enlivening young teenagers had turned the clock back for many of the high-flying passengers. During the spontaneous diversion of pillow throwing they had ignored all their pretenses for the six-hour journey and had willingly revisited their childhood. They had gazed into a time mirror recalling the joyfulness of being a teenager again.

However, I certainly know that our escapades on the plane

back then would never be tolerated on an airline today. There would have been an air marshal on board to immediately stop any fun from breaking out. Boy, I sure miss the good old days of more fun and less stress during airline travel.

After gathering our luggage, we boarded a private bus that took us into Manhattan and to another hotel. There would be neither the opportunity nor the desire to occupy ourselves with juvenile hijinks at the hotel; we were beyond that stage in our maturity.

Team touring Rockefeller Center roof, seventy stories up.

That evening we checked into our rooms like seasoned pros, ate dinner, then walked the streets of New York in complete awe. Although it was nighttime, the bright lights of Broadway made it appear as though the sun was out. We were wide-eyed and eager to take in the utterly foreign sights. It was like we were on a different planet compared to what we had just left behind on the West Coast. The New York night life was as advertised, and we were inhaling all the glamour and dream-like qualities of the great city. That night we slept with visions of Broadway lights and pillows floating over our heads. It had been an amazing first day and the next would even be better.

It was Saturday, October 6; we were scheduled to experience our first World Series game, which was to be played on the historic Polo Grounds. We were so excited about witnessing our first World Series game that we floated to our seats.

There was good and bad news. The good news was that we were about to view our first World Series game; the bad news was that our seats were so buried in the left field bleachers that you could hardly distinguish the numbers on the players' uniforms. We never asked where our seats might be, we just assumed they would be somewhat better than what we found! We couldn't complain because we hadn't paid for them, but our implicit understanding was that the American Legion would provide championship seats for us.

Joe Maguire complained, "If we were any further away from the field we'd be in Yankee Stadium."

We all quietly whined about our seating arrangements, "Is this the way the American Legion organization treats world champs?" George Anderson argued.

"At least our seats could have been in the same time zone as the game!" quipped Paul Schulte.

Our seats gave a new meaning to the phrase "being out in left field."

You had to be an avid Giant or Yankee fan to sit where we were assembled, because you could barely grasp there was a baseball game in progress. Home plate was so far away that to get there you needed a taxi. As disappointed as we were with our seats, we were still happy to be part of the hoopla of the World Series. We were especially thrilled to be enjoying the ambiance and excitement of the great city of New York.

Being in yet another Major League Baseball park within a month was a big adventure for us. The famous Polo Grounds was legendary in baseball lore as it had been the location of so many renowned matches between some of the best teams in baseball history.

Later when the Giants left for San Francisco, the historic Polo Grounds Stadium was demolished. It was the first loss for Major League Baseball tradition and many more would come. Baseball became big business, and with that everything changed—mostly for the worse—thanks to an iron-fisted player's union and avaricious owners. The game became dominated by people who no longer held that simple love for the game; it was now about money. Sparky Anderson said later in his career, "I can't believe they pay us all this money to play baseball—something we did for free as kids." We have grown men playing a kid's game and being paid millions of dollars! What a joke. Unfortunately, the joke is on us!

Of what we were able to see of the game, it appeared that the Giants had thumped the big bad Yankees 6–2 and had grabbed a 2–1 lead in the series. Whitey Lockman's three-run homer was the only highpoint of the game. The game was neither stimulating nor remarkable, unless you like your baseball devoid of any combat. But then again, no one cared—it was the World Series. We had finally seen our first World Series!

After the game, we went to Leon and Eddie's on Fifty-Second Street, a legendary Manhattan watering hole.

The team having fun at the famous Leon and Eddie's in Manhattan.

The waiter solicited drinks, "What'll it be guys? You're all over twenty-one, right?

"Of course! I'll have a gin and tonic." Billy always jumped in with both feet.

The rest of us, who were going to request soft drinks, saw no resistance and followed suit. We were all seventeen years old or under, so we drank the liquor they served us and loved every drop. However, it didn't matter much that we were served alcoholic drinks because they were purposely watered down to a very low percentage of booze. We were charged for a full ounce of liquor, but our drinks contained less than a quarter of an ounce. We didn't care; we were living the good life in New York City.

The drinks were so expensive that we could only afford one each. Our total bill amounted to $150.00 plus tip for fifteen drinks. However, we eagerly paid the price for future boasting rights.

We had a photo taken of the team—except for Jerry Siegert who wasn't there—sitting and standing around a table with Consolo in the middle, toasting us with his gin and tonic. He proceeded with one of his choice joking toasts, "This great team that won the American Legion World Championship walks into this fancy bar in New York City." We all laughed and the flash bulb lit up the room. I still have that picture proudly hanging in my office with all my other cherished photos.

Game four was scheduled to be played on Sunday, October 7, 1951. However, Mother Nature stepped in and rained on the World Series parade. As it turned out, she did us a big favor. The rained-out game gave us another day to absorb more of New York City's glitz and glamor.

We had an extra free play day to do whatever we wanted, and most of us voted to see the treasured buildings and monuments of the city. That day, we had pictures taken atop the Rockefeller Center observation deck, seventy stories and 850 feet high. More photos were taken in front of St. Patrick's Cathedral and many more on a boat ride to the Statue of Liberty. At the statue we climbed the stairs to the top and looked out the windows of the torch that Lady Liberty held high in her right hand. The boat ride back was quite rough; some of us got sea sick. I was one of the "sailors" who unloaded his lunch to the delight of the appreciative fish.

That night we were guests at Radio City Music Hall, where we were enthralled by the world-famous Rockettes, who danced their pretty little legs off. They moved with such grace and smooth synchronicity that I remember being sexually stimulated after their performance. It didn't take much to get a teenage boy to that point—no pun intended—but their unison leg kicks redefined my impression of sensual dancing.

After their performance, a group of us lined up in a Rockettes dancing formation and tried to duplicate their synchronized leg kicks. This spontaneous lark took place right in the middle of Times Square, and it was orchestrated by none other than Mr. Consolo, who loved to perform at any venue at any time. We received some peculiar stares and some friendly encouragement from people on the street. Some spectators joined the fun but during a leg kick, tripped and fell laughing. We all loved the attention and the interest the people of Broadway bestowed on us, especially Billy. When we got back to our hotel, we were exhausted and had had enough New York City life for one day. We slept well that night, dreaming of perfectly proportioned women performing with perfectly shaped Rockette legs.

The next morning, we got our wake up calls in time for the rescheduled game four of the World Series. When we arrived at the Polo Grounds, the American Legion people had us on the playing field posing for pictures and schmoozing with the Giants and Yankees. Some of us had group pictures taken with big leaguers. And our team photo was shot in front of home plate with a large banner we were hanging onto that read, "American Legion—1951—Junior Baseball Champions."

When the game started, we were back in our long distance seats, straining our eyes to see the tiny figures on the field. The game had a historic moment when Joe DiMaggio hit the last homerun of his Hall of Fame career, a three-run shot, and the crowd gave him a rousing standing ovation. At the time, because I was missing the Di from my surname, I didn't know I might be distantly related to Joe. His homerun helped the Yankees beat the Giants 5–2, tying the series at two games each. Except for Joe's homerun, the game was rather lackluster, and we left the Polo Grounds a bit dissatisfied.

"Is this all there is to a World Series game?" Joe Maguire questioned.

Spud added to the discontent with, "I don't see any difference between a regular game and a World Series game." For some reason we expected a lot more than we got.

It was our first hint of disillusionment with overly glorified events that didn't match our expectations. It was a loss of innocence for a bunch of young boys who still believed in the tooth fairy.

We discovered it was much more fun playing and winning a "junior" World Series than watching a "real" World Series game from a mile away. Partaking in life will always override being a voyeur—what a meaningful lesson to learn as a young, untainted teenager. That night we toured the great city of New York for the last time. We attended a live TV program telecast from the Columbia Broadcasting System (CBS) studio Number 50 at Times Square on Broadway. The show was *This Is Show Business*, which was sponsored by Lucky Strike cigarettes.

This would be our concluding evening in New York City, and our dream trip was approaching its final inning. We had rounded the bases and were now heading for home. This time home plate was back on the West Coast where our lives would never be the same.

The next day, October 9, we flew out of New York—exhausted, but with greater wisdom and maturity! We truly appreciated the chance to live our dream, thanks to the opportunity given to us by the American Legion. We continue to thank those great men every day.

The Yankees, as a matter of habit, won the World Series in six games, but by that time we had returned home and we didn't much care. Besides, the Yankees weren't the winners as far as we were concerned. We were the winners, gaining life experience, personal growth, and lifelong friendships as youthful American Legion ballplayers. Our lives had changed for the better, and we could never return to our immature state—we were now men!

Members of the team reunion, Sedona, 2003

Reminiscing, Reuniting, Recounting

SITTING LAZILY ON THE RED Sedona sandstone, we finished our packed lunches around one o'clock and sat chatting among ourselves about what was new in our private lives. We stored the remains of our lunches in trash bags. After a while, I steered the topic back to our main purpose for being there, Billy Consolo.

It was now early afternoon and the bright sun was directly overhead in the high desert of Arizona. All the red rock formations glistened around Secret Mesa as if they had just been washed by a sudden rain. The views were beyond compare. Tourists flocked here on their way to the Grand Canyon only to later find the views there not as inspiring as in Sedona.

The men had loved visiting Sedona since our first reunion celebrating our fiftieth anniversary in 2001, which was held at my home on a Sedona golf course. We had four days of partying, golfing, playing poker, eating, and an abundance of storytelling, which included many jokes. The main storyteller and jokester was, of course, Billy Consolo, and he was a pro! Billy would entertain us by the hour and had us all captivated and laughing until tears came to our eyes. He was totally in his element when he took the floor. No one could do it better. No one bothered trying!

One of his infamous baseball stories was about when Billy had hit a homerun off of Hall of Fame pitcher Bob Feller. It was when Feller was in the twilight of his career and Billy was at his apex. Nevertheless, it upset Feller to the extent that he had a few "well-chosen-words" for Billy as he rounded the bases. Feller said something like, "You lucky little dago bastard! You could never have touched me when I was your age."

But Billy, the quintessential class act, never uttered a word in retort. Knowing that Rapid Robert would be a future Hall of Fame inductee, he wanted to show the respect due. That was Billy Consolo at his best. He could beat you with his bat, his glove, or his legs, but he never flaunted his great gifts or showed egotistical disrespect toward anyone. He would just give you that winning Consolo smile while he was beating your metaphorical brains out with his mind-boggling ability.

As for the validity of Billy's baseball tales, we never questioned the accuracy of his word. We loved Billy. We loved his stories and we didn't care how truthful they were. We wanted more of them.

However, George "Sparky" Anderson offered his own take on Billy's penchant for the truth when he said, "When people ask me if Billy's stories are true, I tell them that you can only believe 5 percent of what you read in the papers or see on TV, but in the case of Billy's stories you can cut that in half."

They loved to rib each other, which dated back to their childhood together. But George knew in his heart that Billy only spoke the truth.

Like Casey Stengel before him, Anderson spoke in his own amusing, enigmatic dialect of the English language that has endeared him to people all over the world. It was said that Casey Stengel butchered the English language. If that was true then Sparky sliced and diced it. But even as much fun as it was to hear George speak his own version of English, no one could tell a story, hold your attention, or thoroughly amuse you like the affable Consolo. Even the highly entertaining Sparky Anderson took a back seat when Billy was in the spot light. He was in a class by himself.

Those of us who loved him couldn't speak for the validity of his voluminous stories, but we hung on every word that slipped off his glib tongue. We didn't care if they were two and a half percent or one hundred percent authentic. It was his presentation that captivated us. He was a born actor and comedian who could spellbind you even with mediocre material.

George was a one man show after Billy was gone, so the magic of our Sedona reunions was never to be repeated. After Billy took flight, George, who so much loved visiting Sedona, couldn't return to the location where they had experienced so much joy together. He said that it would be particularly upsetting for him. However, for just this one day, George had reappeared in Sedona minus Billy for this final show of loyal love for his old co-coach and soul brother.

One of the more delightful events we looked forward to during the reunions was when we were interviewed by Tom and Mike Tabback on the local family-owned radio station KAZM. They featured us on their popular sports talk show every year.

George and Billy interviewed by Mike Tabback of KAZM radio in Sedona

The team after being interviewed by KAZM Sedona radio station, 2003

The station won an award for one of our interviews entitled "Our Love of the Game." Over the years they had emphasized that playing sports for the love of the game was the purest form of any athletics. Owners Tom and Mike Tabback espouse this theory even though their radio station makes a lot of money broadcasting the Arizona Diamondbacks, a professional baseball franchise.

They also were impressed with the level of bonding our team had maintained over the years and the way we related to each other. They continue to insist that what we accomplished beyond playing baseball—lifelong relationships—was what sports is all about, not making millions of dollars!

We had a total of five annual reunions and each was better than the last, until Billy abruptly left the party. How could you throw a party when the life of the party was not in attendance? Without Billy, there was no reunion—no party, no golf, no interviews, nothing, zero. It would be like going to a wedding without the bride and groom present.

So now the party was over, and we were gathered for one day

to remember and pour out our love for William Consolo. We were all back in Sedona just to say good-bye to the man who had left us and took the party with him.

It was time for the Quiet Man to speak up about his relationship with Billy Consolo. We called Bill Lachemann the quiet one because he didn't talk a lot unless spoken to; even then he gave one word answers. Lach, as we also called him, was our catcher and a tough one. He was built like a catcher should be—stocky with a large lower body. When he blocked the plate, the gate was shut; no one got through. Like most catchers with thick legs, he was a very slow runner, but he could really swing a bat.

He was the oldest of three boys, and his two younger brothers had been our batboys. Later in their baseball careers both his kid brothers managed in the major leagues. Marcel Lachemann managed for the Anaheim Angels, and Rene Lachemann managed for the St. Louis Cardinals. Our other batboy, Jimmy Lefebvre, Benny's son, later managed for the Chicago Cubs. So, including Hall of Fame manager George "Sparky" Anderson, that put four members—if you count the batboys—of our team managing in the big leagues. Not a bad record for a bunch of kids off a 1950s Los Angeles playground.

Bill Lachemann had a distinguished coaching career of his own after playing Minor League Baseball for ten years. He was a bullpen coach with the Anaheim Angels and worked with the catchers when his brother Marcel managed the Angels. He lived in Montana and loved to hunt and fish in the surrounding beautiful mountains. He drove to Sedona to pay his homage and respect for Billy C.

"I wanted to be here today because I loved Billy, and, although I said good-bye to him at his funeral, that was for the man. Today is for Billy the ballplayer, to salute him for how he changed all of our lives as our teammate and our brother. With him as our leader, we were a great team. With him, we were better human beings for having known him. With him, we were carried to heights we never imagined, and, with him, we laughed a million times. Without him, we must fight off the grief and carry on as he would have wanted."

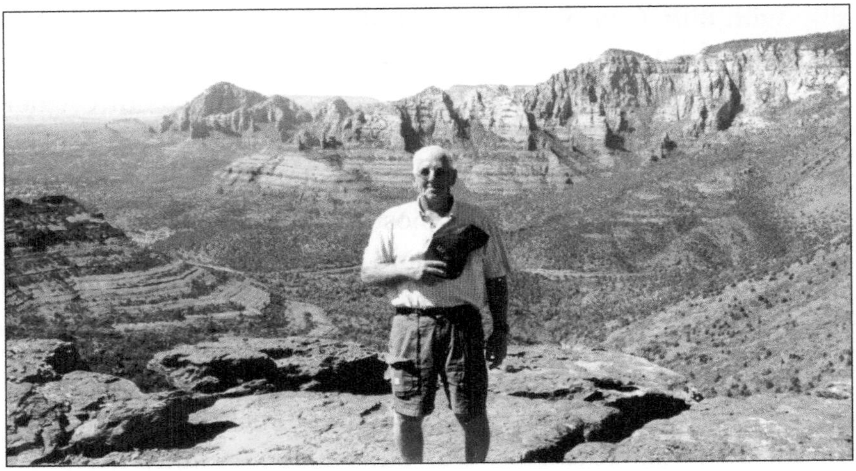

Bill Lachemann

Lach took a few steps forward to move out of the rays of the sun, which were now in his eyes. Although the sun was bright where we were, there were monsoon clouds moving closer in the distance. Could there be rain in our immediate future?

Lach continued, "Usually I'm not good at this speaking thing, but when it comes to talking about Billy the words are flowing. We're not here to cry for Billy, although I could. We're here to laugh with him, because I assure you he's up there somewhere, laughing at us right now." Smiles and a few chuckles broke out among the men in the circle. Lach was right! Billy would be laughing and pointing his index finger at us. With that, the Quiet Man had broken his silence.

Our talented leftfielder was Don Kenway, who could hit, pitch, run, and play with anyone on our team. Don was, in my opinion, the most underrated player on a team where Consolo and Frank Layana got most of the press for their obvious, flashy play. Don

Kenway went about doing his job as our leftfielder with quiet and productive efficiency, doing all the right things at all the right times, like hitting and pitching in the clutch. He wasn't called on to pitch much during the season because Frank and Paul carried the load, but when called upon, it was always in tough situations, and he always performed with great skill. He was the kind of guy who came to work, quietly did his job well, and then went home unnoticed for his fine work. He was one of my favorite teammates because he laughed a lot and always had a smile on his face. Don and his wife, Judy, now live in Farmers Branch, Texas. And, like Bill Lachemann, he wasn't much of a conversationalist, but, when he did speak, you listened because he always had something insightful to convey to us.

Don jumped up from his seat on the sandstone and talked about the fun of knowing Billy Consolo. "Billy could make me laugh just by looking at me. He was a charismatic man when it came to making people feel happy. I think his goal in life was to play baseball at a higher level and to make people laugh, and he did both very well. Billy was always there when we needed him; he came through in the clutch when we needed it and never failed us."

Don Kenway

Don was a schoolmate of Billy's at Dorsey High School in south central Los Angeles, along with ten other team members. Four other members went to Loyola High. Another one opted to go to Hamilton High. Back in the 1940s and '50s you went to the school in the district you lived in, unless you went to Loyola High School, a Catholic School. So, although some of us lived in the same neighborhood, five of us went to different high schools than the other eleven.

Don had more to say as he pointed to the oncoming dark

clouds. "Looks like we're in for some damp weather conditions … I first met Billy in grammar school at Thirty-Ninth Street School and then on to Audubon Junior High. He was always the best athlete at any school he attended, but he never flaunted it. He was the fastest, the strongest, the smartest at whatever sport he attempted to play. You could make up a game and Billy would beat you at it. There wasn't anything he couldn't do when it came to sports. I will miss his humor, his leadership, and his wide smile." Don had no more to say.

The sun had now completely departed and was hidden above some dark threatening monsoon clouds. It looked like it was about ready to drop some serious H_2O at any time. But you never knew when it came to monsoons. They can look very menacing one moment and then move on without a drop of water. It was around 3:00 PM, but the darkened clouds made it seem later than it actually was.

Before the clouds gave some relief, the sun had baked us into an intoxicated altered state that only booze or drugs could otherwise produce. We were tired and wrung out emotionally from a day of spiritual and conscious awakening concerning Billy's departure. We had brought enough food and water to sustain us for the day, but the sun had done a number on our mental and physical energy. We had not bargained for a day like today, nor had we known what an effect it would have on us.

Even I, who had organized this unique gathering, was surprised at the toll it had taken on everyone. Although I was a weather-beaten veteran when it came to the Arizona sun, I was also feeling the adverse effects of it.

Now the sun was gone and the cool breeze on the men's bodies reawakened their senses, so that they might hear the remaining two speakers—Guy McElwaine and me. I had purposely scheduled myself last as I wanted to do something expressively climactic at the end, although I didn't know exactly what it would be at the time.

In 1951, Guy McElwaine was the youngest player on the team at fifteen years old, and the two-year difference between fifteen and seventeen was significant in baseball maturity and strength. He may have only been fifteen, but Guy had the arm strength, baseball skills, self-assurance, and swagger to overcome any age difference. He knew that he could play with ballplayers two years older than he and so did Benny Lefebvre; that's why he picked him over older athletes.

He had irresistible, boyish good looks that attracted flocks of female attention while we were traveling with the Legion team. We were always happy to have him around us because he was a magnet for girls, and, even at fifteen, he had the confidence to approach them.

Upon completing some time in professional baseball after leaving high school, Guy went to Hollywood where he did very well. He succeeded first as an actor, then as an agent, then a producer, and finally a studio CEO. He had the privilege of rubbing elbows with some of Hollywood's elite celebrities, such as Frank Sinatra. In fact, for years he had dated Sinatra's younger daughter, Tina Sinatra. Today he still had the good looks and charisma of an actor, so he could easily handle this speaking assignment.

However, this one would be challenging because as he would say, "I really didn't know Billy that well. I met him the day I was chosen to play on the Legion team. Of course, I knew him by reputation. He was a unanimous All-City pick at third base, and he was the most heralded high school ballplayer to come along in years. I hadn't seen his tremendous talent in person, so playing on the same team with him was an honor and a treat. My first year playing high school baseball was with Hamilton High, and we played against Dorsey and Billy. It was Billy's senior year, and he killed us with his bat and glove. He was the City Player of the Year, and among the voters it was no contest."

Guy was an extremely busy Hollywood executive and hadn't been able to attend any of our five reunions at my house in Sedona.

However, we kept him abreast of what was happening by phone. We would call him sometimes in the middle of an important staff meeting, and he would excuse himself and chat with us for a while. He always took our calls no matter what he was doing.

"I was young and cocky when I played American Legion baseball and when I saw how Consolo conducted himself with all his superior skills, I modeled myself after him, and I became more humble. As a human being you couldn't emulate anyone better than Billy Consolo. He was a class act all his life and that's the highest compliment I can give anyone. I just wish that I had known him better."

Paul Schulte, Jerry Siegert, Billy Consolo, and Warren "Spud" Johnson golfing in Sedona, 2003

The team's first reunion in Sedona, 2001

18

Gone but Not Forgotten

A FEW YEARS BEFORE THE MEMORIAL, as the fiftieth anniversary of our victorious deed approached, I decided to host a reunion at my home in Sedona, Arizona. I figured Sedona would be a great location since it is a vacation spot and tourist attraction in its own right. It boasts stunningly beautiful natural scenery and some fantastic golf courses, which I knew the guys would love. Besides, the decades had slipped away so quickly, and we needed to grab ahold of time while we still had the chance. Although our bonds had remained strong throughout the ups and downs of life, it was time to get together to play and laugh one more time.

It was 2001—a whole new century in a world full of gadgets and gizmos that our seventeen-year-old minds would never have imagined. I carefully planned out a healthy menu I knew the guys would love and that would express my love to them—prime rib and grilled chicken healthfully seasoned with fresh herbs and spices; a bright, colorful salad with light dressing; and freshly made potato salad. Martha Stewart herself would have been envious of my table settings, which included little nostalgic reminders of our times together along with a baseball glove that overflowed like a cornucopia with golf balls and baseballs.

I spent hours preparing a display board with all the newspaper clippings and photos that I could find depicting our days together during our triumphant season. There were articles tracing all of our games on the road as well as coverage of our final win. There were black and white pictures of us taking in the adventure—swimming in Arizona, observing a session of the California legislature, gathering in that bar in New York City.

When the guys arrived at my home, we exchanged our hugs and pats on the back and got down to the business of reminiscing. The guys gravitated to the board, looking at the old images of themselves as they remembered—and misremembered—the details of those glory days. Billy especially, true to form, loudly insisted upon apocryphal exaggerations of what had actually occurred. We didn't mind at all and were more than happy to let his version of the facts stand unchallenged in his mind.

Billy and George, of course, sat together, two sides of the same coin, as had always been the case. We were all now in the latter half of our sixties. George, of course, had looked sixty since he was thirty years old with his prematurely white hair, but age was now also catching up to Billy and his dark Italian hair was now frosted white at the temples. The faces, as far as I was concerned, still all looked the same, in spite of jowls and wrinkles, because the lights in their eyes shown as brightly as ever.

I flitted around the party like a mother hen, making sure that all needs were met and all faces were smiling. But I'd always keep my ear open for Billy's voice, not wanting to miss a bit of his entertaining oratory. Billy jabbered on, hardly getting a bit of food in his mouth, while George listened and ate with intense precision. Every once in a while, George would squeeze a phrase in between the short pauses in Billy's storytelling, correcting him or giving him his opinion in his straight forward, down-to-earth way.

George was always short and to the point in his speech, allowing Billy to get back quickly to the business of bullshitting.

In the days that ensued, we took in a round or two of golf. Some guys still had the old athletic magic, able to swing to hit the ball long and straight. Billy especially, having worked as golf teacher, showed that his athletic gifts had not subsided. Others showed their age with weak, way-over-par performances. But it didn't matter. We were all together again, reliving old memories and making new ones.

The guys loved the fiftieth anniversary reunion so much that we decided to do the same every year ... that is until the reunions came to an abrupt end. In 2008, Billy suddenly and unexpectedly died of a massive heart attack, something we never would have imagined happening, given his unending athletic prowess. After that, it was like the bond between all of us diminished and the reunions simply couldn't and didn't happen. The last time we would gather in Sedona, it would be to say our last good-byes to Billy on that mesa near Cathedral Rock.

Of course, I'd call to keep in touch with the guys, but we were never all together in one place again. I'd call George and encourage him to come visit me in Sedona. He'd just say simply, "I can't, Carl. I just can't." I didn't press him to come because I knew Sedona contained George's last memories of a friendship that few of us are lucky enough to have in a lifetime. Billy had been his rock—through childhood, through Major League Baseball, through life—and now that rock had been suddenly and cruelly washed away by the tides of time.

George had indeed looked like an old man most of his life with his snowy white hair and curmudgeonly features. But those who knew George knew that, in spite of his aged appearance, there was a spunky, indomitable boy who lived inside of him right under the surface. Interface with George for two minutes, especially if you were talking baseball, and the boy would emerge. But, now, bereft of his lifelong friend, he really did begin to age. George was crushed by Billy's death, and it seemed like only his shell remained. It seemed like that boy, George's true spirit, decided, as usual, to tag along with Billy to wherever he had gone in the great hereafter.

Before our eyes, we all watched George Anderson decline, his mind giving way to the ravages of dementia. He even made an attempt to attend a Cooperstown Hall of Fame event, but those who were there knew that the old Sparky was not entirely in attendance. A little more than two years after Billy's death, we lost George. Our stars had both burned out, and our team was now irrevocably undone—at least in this earthly sphere. There was no way that team could have been what it was without the talent and drive of Billy and George, and now they were gone forever.

So here I am, the one left behind in Sedona with those final memories all to myself. Sedona is a popular place to retire and, thus, a good place to look at the realities of life in the face as old age will have you do. The reunions won't ever happen again, although they happen in my mind all the time. I can see all the guys gathering in my home for one last hoorah. I can see Billy's magnificent play every time I look at the green golf courses, and I can see George's caricatured features carved into the red rock formations. They are all here with me, and, yet, at the same time, they are not.

The high desert monsoons especially bring back memories to me of that last time we were together on that mesa, to the moments when I offered my last respects to Billy. I can see George's face, his streaming tears washed away by the big monsoon raindrops. I can feel our last embrace as a team, bonded forever through time.

And I can be transported even further back by the monsoon rainfall, to those times as a kid when we kept on playing in spite of the rain. Rain would not flush us off the baseball field; only darkness would force us to our homes for dinner. After playing in the California downpour for hours, we would head home, riding our bikes in the twilight, sopping wet and mud-covered but with gigantic smiles on our faces.

After dinner, I would take my bat to the backyard and create a movie scene in my head where I was the star, narrator, and hero of an imaginary ballgame. I would swing at nonexistent balls while broadcasting a heroic ninth inning ending of a game. I would supply all the sound effects, including the crack of the bat and the roaring crowd.

"The bases are loaded with two outs. The score is tied in the bottom of the ninth inning. Coming to the plate is Carl Maggio ... Here comes the pitch." I would swing my bat at an imaginary ball and supply the sound effects. "CRACK! It's a long drive to right field. It's going, going, gone!" I would throw my bat aside and hold my arms up triumphantly. "It's a grand slam homerun!" I would go into a homerun trot, creating the sound of approval from the roaring crowd. "The game is over! We win! We win!"

That game-winning homerun was probably my third that week, thanks to the passion of my imagination. However, on one occasion, I flied out for the final put-out, and we lost the game. I had directed the scene and acted it that way since I was getting a big head, winning all those games. I needed to rest my ego's over-inflated self-image.

Playing baseball was all we wanted to do, all day and night, even when it was time to wash the dishes after dinner. It was our passion, and that's what summer was all about. It was our love for the game that kept pushing us to improve, to become more evolved ballplayers.

When you get to the other end of life, you have a whole different perspective on what is real in this world. We had proven that fantasies can indeed come true in this world, and George and Billy had also proven it with their major league careers. When we were seventeen, that championship was as real as anything could get. It meant we were the best team, bar none. That was about all that mattered to us, and it was completely beyond our comprehension that we would one day be looking back on those days fifty or sixty years later. Looking at those old pictures of us is a little like looking at ghosts. You look at yourself at that age and think, "Where did that guy go? Who is that? Who am I now?"

And yet, something does remain that at seventeen you far too easily take for granted. It's really not the championship or the exciting adventures. It's the guys who go along with you for the ride that matter, the friendships and the love that grows over time. Championships can be forgotten, and baseball stars can fade from view. There is nothing tangible about that bond that will stand in a record book, and there is nothing about it I can prove real in scientific terms. Some might call it sentimental delusional nonsense, but I know it in my heart to be true. All those guys are with me and always will be.

Back at that mesa I was the last to speak, to have my "ups," as you would say in baseball lingo. As I stood to speak, the wind started to blow harder and the sky became much darker, which meant monsoon clouds would soon dump their wet load on us already beat up and worn out old guys. The question was, "Could we survive one more tribute without getting soaking wet?" Maybe the monsoon would miss us or maybe not!

American Legion feat sparks Anderson

USA Today 5/2/01

By Bob McManaman
The Arizona Republic

SEDONA, Ariz. — When he was a manager, Sparky Anderson had a sign he kept in his office. "Always believe in miracles," it read.

He had it in Cincinnati, where he guided the Big Red Machine to four pennants and two World Series titles. He had it in Detroit when he and the Tigers cruised to the crown in 1984.

He had it in his heart, too, years earlier, when he and 15 other neighborhood kids from Los Angeles managed to do something pretty magical. To Anderson, it was bigger and better than any World Series in the big leagues.

Fifty years ago, they won the American Legion national championship.

"The most exciting season in my life was that one back in '51, on that American Legion team," he said. "Yes, I was fortunate enough to go on from there and win a lot of other things, but that year was still the best, and I'll tell you why.

"Because those were some of the best guys I ever played with. We grew up together. We learned the game together. We were best friends, and that's never changed."

This week, Anderson and many of his teammates from Crenshaw Post 715 are in Arizona to commemorate their victory. They're celebrating the 50-year anniversary of the championship with a reunion in Sedona at the home of teammate Carl Maggio. They've come from California, from Texas, and even as far away as Bangkok for the weeklong celebration.

Photo by Reed Saxon, AP

Diamond jubilee: Sparky Anderson says 50th anniversary of American Legion title is special.

"I wouldn't have missed it for the world," said Frank Layana, one of the team's pitchers, who flew in from Thailand. "Most of us have all kept in touch over the years." Maggio, an outfielder for Crenshaw, is hosting the event along with another former teammate, Warren "Spud" Johnson of nearby Prescott.

About a dozen made the trip, and the reunion will include a few rounds of golf, a tour through the Sedona area and more than a few bull sessions about baseball and the summer of '51.

"Most of us have known each other since we were 7, 8, 9 years old," Maggio said. "We played on the same sandlot together as kids. That one year, it all came together for us."

The tournament had more than 2,000 teams. Crenshaw captured it by defeating a club from White Plains, N.Y., in the final at Detroit's Briggs Stadium, which later became Tiger Stadium.

"Ironic, isn't it?" said Anderson, who played shortstop for Crenshaw.

He might be the most famous member of the team, but others left their mark. A half-dozen of them signed pro deals, including third baseman Bill Consolo, who played briefly with Boston.

The team's bat boys did even better. Three of them — Jim Lefebvre and brothers Marcel and Rene Lachemann — managed in the majors. Lefebvre's father, Benny, coached the team. The Lachemanns' older brother Bill was the catcher.

"It was a special group of guys," said Anderson, who then was known as "Georgie."

"He didn't have the nickname Sparky yet," said Layana, whose son Tim pitched in the majors. "My dad always talked about him. He'd tell me, 'You need that spark, just like Georgie has.'

"You know, now that I think about it, maybe that's how the nickname got started."

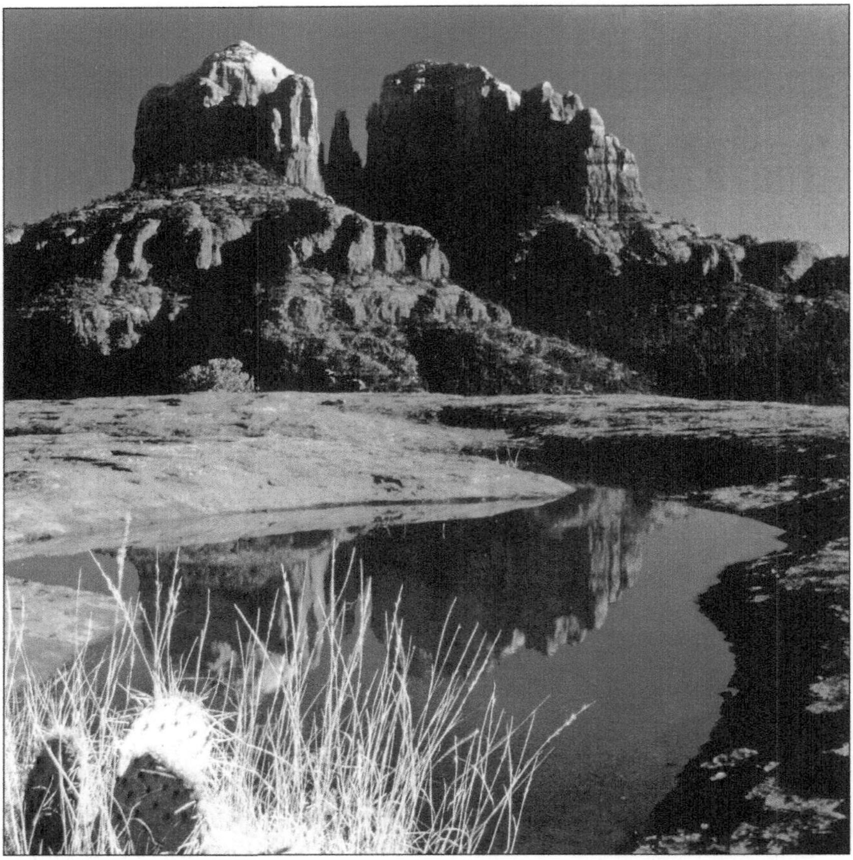

I shouted out, "Billy is with us...Let's all be conscious of his spirit...
Billy was and always will be Superman...
Let's all welcome Superman back to Sedona!"

19

LETTING GO WITH LAUGHTER

AS OUR EULOGIES TO BILLY neared conclusion, the monsoon clouds hung directly overhead. The wind swirled around Secret Mesa, blowing dust everywhere. Was there any doubt that we were in for some rain? It was not cold, as the temperature was about 78 degrees Fahrenheit, so there was no need for jackets. However, no one was prepared for rain, so getting wet was a possibility.

As I stood in the middle of the circle of these mature, hard-baked old guys, I couldn't help but experience vivid flashbacks to when we were teenagers. Back then, we played on the streets and playgrounds of Los Angeles with no worries or issues to weigh us down. The one common bond that held us together was our mutual love for the game of baseball. We knew that if there was someone out there with a bat and ball in his hand we would find him and play some ball. It never mattered to us who a kid's parents were, what religion he chose, or the color of his skin. So long as we had two boys, a bat, and a ball, all of our problems were solved as far as we were concerned.

Every one of us now had legitimate issues, whether they were related to finance, family, or health. Those of us who had extra income helped the guys who had fallen on hard times. One of our teammates was ill and had very little cash flow. We all contributed in his time of need, and he appreciated it. No one on our team was going to live with unpaid bills or without enough food. Charity began at home with family, and family included our teammates. It was all for one and one for all. We became a cohesive family unit, and we will be until there are none of us left on the planet.

But today we were all together for only one reason—to honor and praise a fallen old friend and to learn some conscious lessons about life, death, and how closely the two are related as one grows older. One day a person is with us, the next day he or she is gone! What is that all about? How do you deal with it? Maybe today, as a group, we could expose some veiled evidence to logically unravel the puzzle. Now it was my task to bring everyone together as one through our last hurrah to Billy, as we sent him our loving thoughts.

From my spot in the middle of the circle, I took a deep breath and closed my eyes, concentrating on how my oration might complement the nine speakers before me. I wanted to bring this transformative day to an emotionally uplifting conclusion. My teammates were counting on it!

I exhaled and felt the first drop of rain hit my face. I laughed and thought, "Billy is setting me up for his final ruse of the day, using rain for another one of his practical jokes." Some would have suggested that the sprinkle was a coincidence, but I knew it was not a coincidence. For me it was proof that Billy was with us. It was his way of saying, "Yes, I'm here and thanks for gathering to show your love for me, and, here, take this drenching for your trouble." I giggled under my breath. "Oh, it is Billy, alright! He always had the last laugh or pulled the final prank."

I started speaking, hoping that the words would spill out smoothly and coherently and that they would tumble together in a meaningful, poignant finale.

"Billy was a man's man, and males of all ages gravitated to his charismatic persona, wanting to bond with him, and I was no exception. I first met Billy in about the fourth grade when we were eight or nine years old. It was instant chemistry with the two of us, and we knew that we were meant to be good friends. We attended different grammar schools; he attended Thirty-Ninth Street School and I attended Transfiguration Grammar School. However, Billy was part of a group from public schools that came to my church for religious instruction. We were studying to receive our First Holy Communion and Confirmation together, and after about four months of spiritual instruction, we went through the religious ceremony on a Sunday afternoon. We opened ourselves to the spiritual experience and felt 'holy' for it. And then we argued about who was the 'holiest of holies.' 'You're full of holes, alright,' he would tell me.

"After that spiritual bonding, we reunited on the playground, playing baseball together for a couple years. Then when we were thirteen years old, we played on a Midget League team together with all the other boys our age in the neighborhood. That playground team was called the Terrors, and we won the Los Angeles City Championship in 1947.

"Billy was like a brother to me, and he had celebrity status. In my eyes he was a star and not just because of his loftier baseball abilities. His whole persona had star features. He was someone we all looked to for leadership and direction. Billy always knew who he was and was conscious of what his mission was on this planet. We studied his magnetic appeal so that we might somehow find the missing parts of ourselves. We tried to emulate him not only as a ballplayer but also as a gifted human being. He was a super talent, not only as an athlete. He also had a special gift for making people laugh. Billy loved to laugh and generate a gleeful response from other people. His stories were endless, entertaining, and we never wanted them to stop! Unfortunately for us, they did stop when he left us. But, like his stories, he will live on in our hearts and memories. This is a man that we will never forget, and he will be in our conscious thoughts daily."

I hesitated and thought, "Is this all I can include in the closing stages of this memorable day?" As I looked into the exhausted and glassy eyes of my teammates, I knew it was enough.

The rain fell harder on the sacred little plateau of red rock, but we hardly noticed the wet stuff. The pools of water around us were rough with wind and the splattering of rain. The reflection of Cathedral Rock could not be seen in any of the pools as was usually the case. There were flashes of lightning overhead followed by claps of thunder, which confirmed that a monsoon had engulfed us. The rain was now coming down in sheets. The strange part of it was that no one seemed to care! No one considered running for cover. There was no shelter within three hundred yards, and we had parked our vans far away on the dirt road. We had spent most of the day under the warm desert sun sweating; now the cool monsoon rain refreshed us.

I fought back the tears, knowing that our time was running out on Secret Mesa. Yet, no one was making a move to leave. Nothing would push us off the monsoonal mesa until we completed our quest to fulfill the purpose for which we were gathered. I looked into the eyes of my teammates, and they stared back at me, waiting for me to do something inspiring as a finale.

I was much too tired to think, so I let my instincts take over, and words flowed out of my mouth like someone else was speaking them. I couldn't wait to hear what I had to say!

I shouted over the rain, "Billy is with us. Let's all be conscious of his spirit. Billy was and always will be Superman. Let's all welcome Superman back to Sedona!"

I was becoming a little too esoteric, but I couldn't help myself. It was the way I usually feel after about three martinis, if I can still stand up—in a unique conscious and spiritual realm.

We all knew Billy was there. We could feel his teasing influence. He was looking down on us, snickering at our soaked bodies. The thought of him laughing at us made me chuckle out loud. Making me laugh was something he had done many times before. Now I had a joke for him.

I looked up into the crying sky. Rain was running off my face. Pointing my finger skyward, I yelled to the heavens, "Over the years you've told us hundreds of jokes. Now I have one for you. Superman walks into this bar in heaven, and six of his American Legion teammates are sitting at the bar having a beer ... and there's an empty barstool."

That gag invigorated the fatigued, timeworn males, instantly radiating them with energetic, animated vitality. The old guys started laughing, and they forced themselves up off the sandstone. With the rain dripping off our faces, we began dancing and hugging each other while yelling, crying out with tears of delight, and laughing loudly. Our bodies were comingled in a football type huddle; we were bouncing in unison to the rhythm of our combined emotions. Our minds had risen to a higher, more resilient level of functionality. We gained greater ability to dissipate the disorder and chaos, which allowed clarity.

Vocalizing our personal, loving thoughts about Billy reminded us of what we loved about ourselves and how much fun it was to be celebrating his life. We were like young boys again—no worries and no issues, just teammates remembering a huge victory in our lives that brought a deeper understanding of Billy's mortality as well as our own. We were in a collective altered state that quelled our resistance to Billy's death. Letting go of the resistance released our pain. We were all drawn into the trance of a gleeful chant.

We all chanted, "SUP-ER-MAN! SUP-ER-MAN! SUP-ER-MAN!"

A highly synergistic energy had risen like a fast foaming glass of champagne; it was now overflowing onto the red rocks. Our seventy-something stiffness seemed to melt away as we stood in a huddled group hug, dancing to the primal beat of our collective souls. Our entangled arms and legs were transported beyond time. We were seventy and seventeen all together at that moment in time, chanting our mantra, "SUP-ER-MAN! SUP-ER-MAN! SUP-ER-MAN!"

We flashed back to 1951 for that split second in a dazed state, romping onto our grass-stained championship dog pile, tasting the sweetness of victory. We were teenagers again, basking in the exhilaration that had taken us from undisciplined sandlot players to world champions. Having transcended the bitterness of our loss of Billy, we were absolutely in the moment as well as completely beyond the grasp of time amid our love for one another.

After fifty-six years, we had all come together, victorious again, this time as an enduring team of old souls and young hearts. It felt warmly familiar and life enhancing for each of us. As the rain pummeled our ecstatic faces, our hearts connected and gathered around our love for William Angelo Consolo and the game of baseball. We reveled in our love for each other and for what we had accomplished together while playing the game we cherished—as kids, friends, and teammates in that miraculous summer of 1951.

Epilogue

OUR CHAMPIONSHIP TEAM WAS LOADED with exceptional athletes who were also great human beings. Every one of us took extreme pleasure in playing baseball for one reason alone—the love of the game. Each game was played with the joy that brings meaning to life every day. The memories we now have of the times spent bonding and playing together are priceless. We wouldn't trade them for all the money in the world. We loved playing baseball and grew to love each other as a family. The bonds that developed between teammates on the baseball diamond stuck with us all of our lives.

Our future family lives included all our old baseball teammates. When any member needed help personally or financially, we were all there to support them. We learned from Benny Lefebvre that turning on our light switches united us as a team and as brothers in life, and we still have our light switches turned on for each other. When the last one of us leaves this earth, he will turn off that last light switch and the stadium will go dark.

The ten surviving team members—nine now that Georgie has joined Billy—have never returned to Sedona as a group. Some visited with their wives and friends, but there was never again the fun-loving, camaraderie that we experienced as a team. With Billy Consolo's death, there was no chance of recapturing the magic. It was like the show was over and the spotlight had been turned off. The death of George "Sparky" Anderson several months later made it clear that the foundation of the team was gone. If the old team would ever be together again, it would have to be on some kind of heavenly playing field in the great beyond.

However, in this life, as long as our minds allow, we always will have the memories of the days we spent together playing, laughing, and loving at our reunions in Sedona. And, of course, we will also always have our 1951 American Legion National Championship season. Time can take our teammates from us, but nothing can take those memories away.

The American Legion was the greatest amateur baseball association ever created in the United States, and our championship had been played during the height of its existence. After the 1951 season ended, other leagues began to form, which leached teams and players away from the American Legion. Never again would there be 16,300 teams in one amateur league competing for a single national championship. Today there are only 5,400 American Legion teams in fifty states, Canada, and Puerto Rico vying for the American Legion championship. Unfortunately, there is now no way to determine which team is the ultimate amateur world champion.

There was only one team that could claim the amateur national championship in 1951, but now there are so many leagues that have their own champions. So who is the best of the best of all these leagues? No one can ever know. There is no playoff system in place, and there never will be because it would take forever to determine a single team champion with all the leagues currently in existence. In 1951, there was no doubt who was the number one amateur team in the country. We were the only ones left standing that summer after playing almost forty games.

What Births a Superior Athlete?

In reading this book before releasing it for publication, I was reminded of some special qualities of my teammates. Of course, all of my fifteen teammates were special, and I loved them all as brothers. However, Billy Consolo and George "Sparky" Anderson were head and shoulders above the rest of us because they were fearless. Fear-based behavior debilitates one's ambitions if you're engaged in competitive sports. Fear saps your life force and tightens your nerves, which is why absolute courage is needed to survive the constant stress of being a top performing athlete. Fear on the baseball field makes mice out of men and turns excellent players into average ones.

Both Billy and George were fearless when faced with game situations that were fear-provoking to most athletes. Many times during the season they were called on to face panic head-on and act courageously based on their ability to stare down fear until it dissipated into thin air. They had the ability to translate chaos into focused consciousness, which shifts the action into slow motion. Playing in such a state allows an edge of fearlessness with release from pressure. This, in my opinion, is what births a superior athlete. It was also why those two teammates played in the major leagues; they were fearless.

Appendix

Crenshaw Post No. 715 . . . 1951 National Champions

Crenshaw Post No. 715 of Los Angeles sponsored the winning combination in the Silver Anniversary session of American Legion Junior Baseball National Finals. Led by a hard playing third baseman, named Bill Consolo, the California entry subdued a stubborn White Plains, New York team in the final game at Briggs Stadium, Detroit, by a score of 11 to 7.

In twenty-five years of American Legion Junior Baseball, the Crenshaw club became the seventh California entry to win top honors. Oakland, who had the crown for 1949 and 1950 lost out in the state playoff this year to Sacramento, and then Sacramento in turn lost to the boys from L. A. Then the Los Angeles club really got down to business and won the National Regional at Winslow, Arizona in straight games, defeating Tucson, Arizona (27-6), Larmington, Utah (7-2), and Tucson again (11-0). In Sectional play at Hastings, Nebraska the boys from Crenshaw continued their winning ways by knocking off Omaha, Nebraska (10-0), Billings, Montana (6-0), and then won again from Omaha in a 13-inning contest, 3 to 2.

At the National Finals, played this year in Detroit's beautiful Briggs Stadium, Los Angeles won their first two games, defeating Jacksonville, Florida (8-4) and Cincinnati, Ohio (1-0). Then they met White Plains, New York in what could have been the final contest, but a determined and persistent White Plains club set the L. A. entry down 3 to 1.

Record of the 1951 Champs:

Los Angeles 27—Tucson, Arizona . . .	6	(Regional No. 12)
Los Angeles 7—Larmington, Utah . . .	2	
Los Angeles 11—Tucson, Arizona . . .	0	
Los Angeles 10—Omaha, Nebraska . . .	0	(Sectional "D")
Los Angeles 6—Billings, Montana . . .	0	
Los Angeles 3—Omaha, Nebraska . . .	2	
Los Angeles 8—Jacksonville, Florida . .	4	(National Finals)
Los Angeles 1—Cincinnati, Ohio . . .	0	
Los Angeles 1—White Plains, New York	3	
Los Angeles 11—White Plains, New York	7	

1951 NATIONAL CHAMPIONS—LOS ANGELES, CALIFORNIA

Co-sponsored by Crenshaw Post No. 715 and Marshall-Clampett Motors

Front Row, left to right: Joe Maguire, Carl Maggio, Frank Layana, George Anderson, William Consolo, Paul Schulte, Warren Appley, Bill Lachemann. *Second row:* Charles Wilson, manager, Gordon Sherrett, Donald Kenway, Bob Morris, Wilfred Zander, John Siegert, Warren Johnson, Guy McElwaine, Melvin Goldberg, Benny LeFebvre, Coach.

1951 NATIONAL RUNNER-UP, WHITE PLAINS, NEW YORK

Co-sponsored by White Plains Post No. 135 and Ramon Motors

Front row, left to right: Donald Huszar, Sam Alston, Anthony Zanazzi, Daniel Breslin, Angelo Belmont, Raymond Gilmore, James Patterson. *Second Row:* Mort Grossman, Coach, George Raimo, Edwin Janecek, Grover Jones, Jr., Jack Yvars, Jr., Dean Loucks, John Perkins, Doane Lydecker, Donald McLean, Harry Rodriques, Manager. *Front:* Robert Pollock, batboy.

Sixteen Player Roster
1951 American Legion World Champions
Coached by Benny Lefebvre

- **Billy Consolo** (Third Base), Los Angeles City Player of the Year from Dorsey High
- **Frank Layana** (Picher-Outfielder), was All-Catholic League and All CIF at Loyola High
- **Paul Schulte** (Pitcher) All-Catholic League from Loyola High
- **Joe Maguire** (Second Base), All-Catholic League at Loyola High
- **Don Kenway** (Outfield-First Base), from Dorsey High
- **Bill Lachemann** (Catcher), from Dorsey High
- **Mel Goldberg** (Outfield-First Base), from Dorsey High
- **Warren Johnson** (Infield-Outfield-Catcher), from Dorsey High
- **Gordy Sherett** (Outfielder), from Dorsey High
- **"Red" Zander** (Pitcher), from Dorsey High
- **Warren Appley** (Outfielder-Infielder), from Dorsey High
- **Bobby Morris** (Outfield-First Base), from Dorsey High
- **Jerry Siegert** (First Base), from Dorsey High School
- **Guy McElwaine**, our fifteen-year-old junior high phenom
- And of course me, **Carl Paul Maggio** (outfield), from Loyola High

Mel Goldberg

Jerry Siegert

Carl Maggio

Bobby Morris

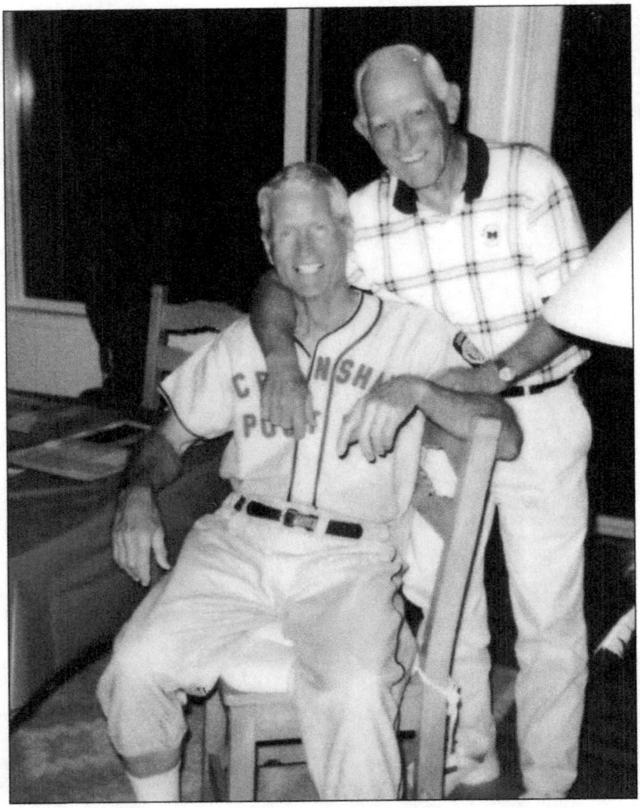

George and Paul in Sedona.
Paul is wearing his original Crenshaw baseball uniform.

Group shot in Sedona

Carl pointing out George's picture
in the Baseball Hall of Fame

Baseball card featuring George "Sparky" Anderson

Joe Magurie, Paul Schulte, Frank Layana, and Carl Maggio, four players from Loyola High School

George "Sparky" Anderson in the Baseball Hall of Fame

Billy Consolo

Paul Schulte

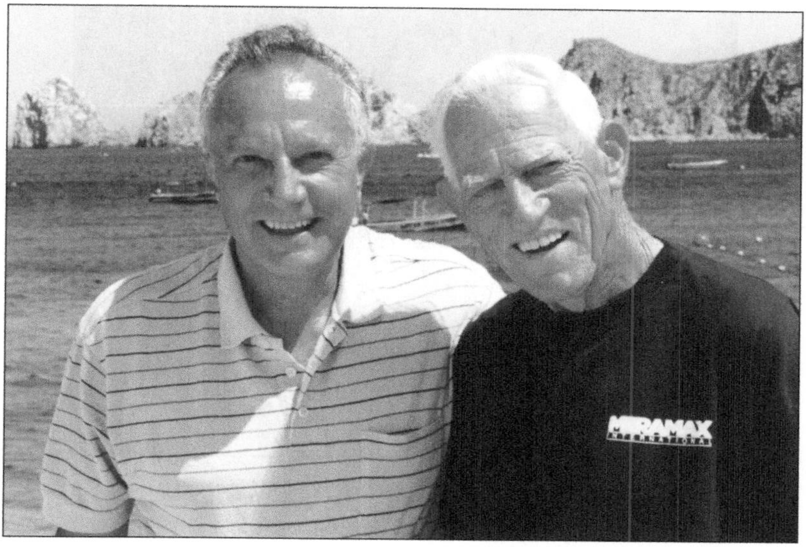

Carl and George in Cabo San Lucas, Mexico

George and Carol Anderson in Cabo San Lucas, Mexico

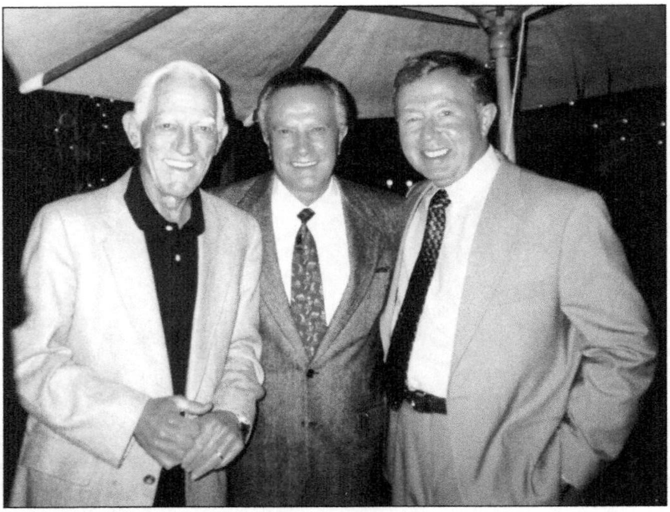

George, Carl, and Tom Seeberg at a party

Sparky sleeping in Sedona

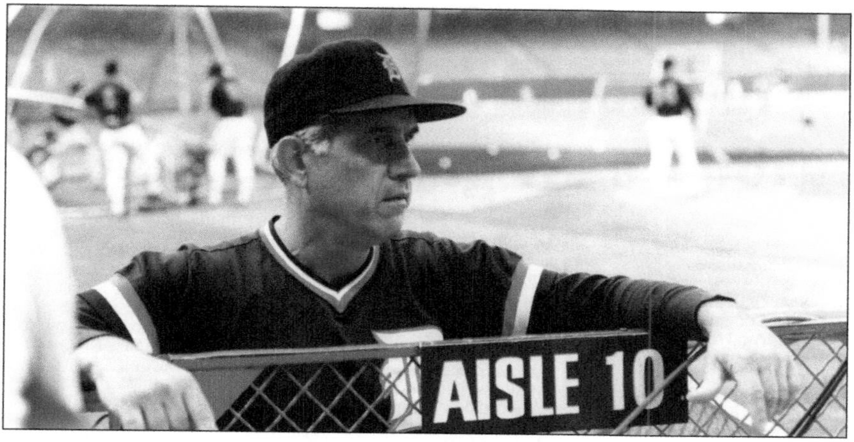

Billy C. playing for the Angels

Frank Layana shakes hands with our sponsor, Fred Clampitt, as George "Sparky" Anderson and Joe Maguire watch

© THE ARIZONA REPUBLIC

Anderson: Work stoppage would cost game too much

By Bob McManaman
The Arizona Republic

Sparky Anderson misses Major League Baseball, but the retired Hall of Fame manager said baseball is missing the boat if it puts its fans through yet another work stoppage next season.

"The game can't afford it. Not now," said Anderson, who is in Sedona this week for a 50-year reunion with former teammates commemorating their victory at the 1951 American Legion national championships.

Anderson, 67, said baseball has rebuilt its reputation in recent years with some incredible individual performances, such as the home run record chase in 1998 between Mark McGwire and Sammy Sosa. But with attendance figures showing signs of fatigue, Anderson is convinced Major League Baseball will permanently lose fans if labor strife puts the 2002 season in jeopardy.

"Baseball is coming back strong, and one thing all of us would agree upon is that the people in charge have to have enough sense not to make the same mistake again," the former manager of the Cincinnati Reds and Detroit Tigers said. "There's plenty (of money) there for both sides to enjoy, and they have to sit down for however long it takes and resolve the situation.

"I really think they can avoid this. I think they've got enough sense. If not, we're in for some pretty serious bad times, in my opinion."

Anderson also said he thinks it's time for Pete Rose, baseball's all-time hits leader, to be inducted into the Hall of Fame.

"I just hope it happens before my time on Earth is up," he said. "Yes, Pete deserves to be in Cooperstown and for one simple reason: You can't have the game's greatest hits man not be in the Hall of Fame. It's time they put him in there. If they don't want to let him put a uniform on again, fine, but don't penalize him."

Anderson said Rose, the heart and soul of teams in Cincinnati, never besmirched baseball during his playing career, and that should be taken into consideration for his reinstatement and eventual election into the Hall.

"Nobody ever talks about this," Anderson said, "but they have all this proof, as they say they do, about what Pete did as a manager and yet, they can never produce anything against him when he was a player. They've got to separate it. What Pete did as a player speaks for itself. Put him in the Hall of Fame where he belongs."

"Yes, I was fortunate enough to go on from there and win a lot of other things, but that year was still the best, and I'll tell you why. ...We were best friends and that's never changed.

Sparky Anderson

Former Reds and Tigers manager on being a member of the 1951 American Legion championship team

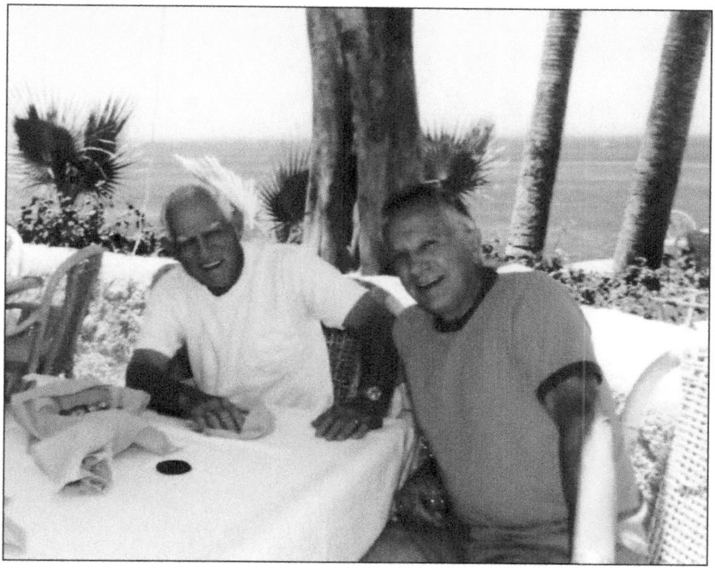

George and Carl living the good life in Cabo San Lucas, Mexico

About the Author

CARL PAUL MAGGIO, RAISED IN southern California, became involved in sports at an early age and honed his skills as a baseball player. He attended the University of Southern California on a baseball scholarship and majored in marketing and business administration. Carl's baseball career also included playing in the Canadian League and during his service in the United States Navy.

The majority of Carl's business career involved his leadership in a major Real Estate Firm in Southern California, where he also trained and motivated staff members.

Carl's interests include acting, both in college movies and in the film industry; and he is an avid, lifetime photographer. He has traveled extensively throughout the world and the United States.

He is most proud of his three grown children and his six beautiful granddaughters.

Carl serves on the board of directors of the University of Southern California Baseball Alumni Association. He is currently retired and lives in Sedona, Arizona.

CPSIA information can be obtained at www.ICGtesting.com
Printed in the USA
LVOW01s0609021013

355044LV00017BA/56/P

9 781627 870030